Soul Survivors

SOUL SURVIVORS

True Stories of
Striving and Yearning

by

HANOCH TELLER

in collaboration with
Marsi Tabak

New York City Publishing Company

Printed in Israel
Typeset by Gefen Ltd.

Library of Congress catalog card number: TX 1-597-322

ISBN 0-961-4772-0-2

Second Edition

15   14   13   12   11   10   9   8   7   6   5   4

Available through:

NYC Publishing Co.
37 W. 37th St. 4th floor
NY, NY 10018

CIS Distributors
P.O.B. 26
Lakewood N.J. 08701

J. Lehmann
Hebrew Booksellers
20 Cambridge Terrace
Gateshead
Tyne & Wear

Kollel Bookshop
22 Muller St.
Yeoville Johannesburg 2198

To the memory of the Maggidim, men whose stories and parables served to uplift, inspire and rebuke generations of our People.

לעילוי ולזכר נשמת מרן הראש ישיבה
הגאון רבנו חיים שמואלביץ זצוק״ל
שר התורה והיראה
אשר זכיתי להסתופף בצילו
ולהיבנות משגב דבריו.

״נישט די מעשים טייצ׳ען אפ דעם מענטשן
נאר דער מענטש טייצ׳ט אפ ד׳ מעשים.״

(לא המעשים מתארים את האדם
אלא האדם הוא המאפיין את מעשיו)
הגר״יח זצוק״ל

APPROBATION FROM HAGAON HARAV SHLOMO ZALMAN AUERBACH SHLITA

הרב שלמה זלמן אויערבאך

פעיה"ק **ירושלים** תובב"א

ב"ה, יום ...

(handwritten Hebrew text)

I hereby express my most heartfelt blessing to my dear friend, Rabbi Hanoch Yonason Teller, who studies in the *Kollel* of the Mirrer Yeshiva. I know him very well and can veritably testify that he is a fearer of sin and a Torah scholar.

Since he is in the category of a *talmid chacham* who does not allow anything improper to emanate from his hands, not to mention knows how to word things pleasantly and correctly, his intention to publish a book of his stories about Torah leaders and loving ones fellow Jew, etc.; in order to strengthen faith in God and enhance mitzva observance for an English reading audience receives my thorough endorsement. I extol his actions and extend my blessings that his words will penetrate the hearts of his readers and influence them to uplift and improve their deeds and purify their outlook for their own everlasting benefit.

May the author be blessed for his efforts from the source of blessing as he so desires, and I so fervently wish.

Shlomo Zalman Auerbach

APPROBATION FROM HAGAON HARAV MOSHE FEINSTEIN SHLITA

RABBI MOSES FEINSTEIN	משה פיינשטיין
455 F. D. R. DRIVE	ר"מ תפארת ירושלים
New York, N. Y. 10002	בנוא יארק
—	
ORegon 7-1222	בע"ה

ב' ניסן תמש"ה

לכבוד מוהר"ר העניך סעללער שליט"א, בברכת שלום וברכה וכט"ס.

אחדשה"ט Due to the delicate state of my health, it is difficult for me to delve into books sent to me for endorsement.

הנה מחמת However, I heard wonderful tidings regarding your most

לפני recent as well as your earlier book, from my grandson

להסכמה, HaRav Mordechai Tendler, Shlita. He praised the books

י הרה"ג as ones which can provide a great service in drawing the

hearts of many of our brethren to their Father in Heaven.

מוהר"ר פ להמשיך לבות Therefore, I offer my blessings that the Almighty will

של הרבה award you with much success with this book, and that

שיצליחן you may merit to increase and glorify the Torah. I have

השי"ח בט instructed that my seal be impressed upon this letter.

Moshe Feinstein

צוחי שישימר הרתמתי על מכחב זה.

Contents

ב"ה

Preface

THERE IS MORE to story-telling than telling stories. The story-teller sees a story where others can fathom no more than a series of seemingly unconnected events, but he has not fulfilled his calling until he has translated what he discerns and perceives into words that can touch the soul. He must pave a highway with those words, a highway to the heart.

A journalist records events he has just witnessed; a historian chronicles entire epochs. If their pens are keen, both the journalist and the historian can paint vivid pictures that evoke lasting images in the mind. But the story-teller aspires to penetrate the soul.

As a medium that can amuse or enlighten, stimulate or sadden, elucidate or uplift, a story plays a manifold role in man's existence. But the capacity of a story to *teach* raises the medium to a higher plane. From among the scores of true stories I heard or witnessed while compiling this anthology, I have culled those which embody an *edifying* lesson and a message that is universal.

The three-strand cord, *Koheles* teaches, will not quickly be severed. Each of the three tales that comprise every chapter in this book constitutes a single strand; together they form a triple-ply cord through which, it is hoped, the message they convey will not quickly be forgotten.

The trilogies tell of the fortitude of our people: men who outshone the Enlightenment; women who overcame the temptations of their time; children who risked everything to escape to *Eretz Yisrael*; and chassidim whose faith was unshakable. Those who withstood the allure of assimilation, those who never succumbed to the seductions of society, those whose lives and deeds are the very essence of the Greatest Story of All — they are the *SOUL SURVIVORS*.

Several years ago I noticed in the unclaimed letter department of Jerusalem's main Post Office a pile of envelopes addressed to God. They were all written in the inimitable handwriting of children. The simple and naive piety of those youngsters left a profound impression. I, too, must commence my acknowledgements with a thank you letter to Hashem for all the kindness bestowed upon me and the ability to complete this work. I also thank all of my *Rebbeim* who share their wisdom and provide such sterling examples — most particularly the Mirrer *Rosh Yeshiva* in whose *kollel* I learn.

There are many people whose assistance, both specifically with this book and more generally over the years, have made the publication of this volume a much easier task than it might have been. Firstly, I would like to express my gratitude to the individuals who told me stories and those who were the stories. Also, I must thank the Hebrew daily *HaModia* for permitting me to adapt two stories which appeared in its pages (under different titles): *Thirst,* by Rabbi Aaron Surasky, and *Promise,* by Ruth Lichtenstein.

I deeply appreciate the suggestions and criticisms offered by Joseph Telushkin, Shimon Glick, Zelda Goldfield and Jonathan and Judith Rosenblum. Their expert advice was surpassed only by their generosity of time in wading through large sections of the manuscript.

My greatest debt of gratitude is extended to MARSI TABAK whose patient ear and gifted pen scrutinized every word of this book. Her felicity of style and virtuosity in graphics is bountifully represented in these pages.

And once again, the wonderful team at *NYC* Publishing deserve special plaudits. My dear parents, who were such help to *Once Upon a Soul* (and its author!), have shown the same enthusiasm for *Soul Survivors*.

As always, I am deeply indebted to my wife, who shares all that I do and all that I am. May the Almighty grant us the privilege of seeing our children and our children's children fulfill the concepts and ideals portrayed in these stories.

Lastly, I wish to thank the ordinary people whose extraordinary stories never made it into this book.

אני תקוה שמילותי ישאו הד בלבות הקוראים.

Hanoch Teller
Jerusalem תשמ״ה
Lag Ba'Omer 5745/May 1985

Introduction

WHY DO PEOPLE tell stories?

I'll tell you a story.

It was a stormy, moonless night and two men – one foolish, the other wise – groped their way through the dark, gloomy forest. With no source of illumination whatsoever, they were hopelessly lost. Suddenly, there was a deafening crash of thunder and a brilliant flash of lightning.

The simpleton looked up to admire the spectacle. The wise man exploited the brief moment of light to get his bearings.

A good story is like a flash of lightning. For some, it is a spectacle fascinating to behold, and, as the glimmer of the spectacle fades, so does all memory of the story. For others, it is a tool to be utilized, a lesson that can light a path through a dark existence. Once employed, the story and its lesson become self-perpetuating.

... As soon as he got his bearings, the wise man guided

his foolish companion to the charred remains of a tree trunk struck by the lightning. Working together, they revived the still-glowing embers and soon they had a blazing campfire going.

All night long, by the warmth of the fire, the wise man told the simpleton the secrets of his wisdom. And when the sun rose the following morning, the simpleton was no longer simple.

This chassidic story is allegorical. Torah narrative, however, is not. It is the history of our People and our Faith. Certainly, the Exodus from Egypt has all the essential elements of a good story: a protagonist, supporting characters, drama, pathos, tension, action, miracles, intrigue — and a magnificent climax. The images it evokes constitute a spectacle fascinating to behold. But it is *not* sufficient that we appreciate the beauty of the story and applaud its superb style, for we are enjoined to retell this story year after year, in minute detail. This in itself emphasizes the story's intrinsic significance.

The object of the Exodus was *Matan Torah* — the presentation of the body of law that is the cornerstone of Judaism. Only by first experiencing the Exodus, could a nation of slaves be made receptive to that vast fount of knowledge. Only by experiencing the Exodus, could a nation of slaves be transformed into a Kingdom of Priests. And only then could God begin teaching them the Torah.

But it was not only the nation newly emancipated from bondage that stood at the foot of Mount Sinai. The souls of all the Children of Israel were present: our own souls were there, and those of our yet-unborn children, and of the generations of our People to come. So that we may be as receptive as our brethren who were present in body, we — the scholarly and the untutored, the affluent and the indigent, the elderly and the toddler, the artisan and the unskilled, the sophisticated and the innocent — must likewise experience the Exodus.

The story is the tool that enables us to relive that experience. The retelling of the story perpetuates its message. And, thus, the souls of the Torah receivers survive...

3

on Providence

גדל העצה ורב העליליה אשר
עיניך פקוחות על כל דרכי בני
אדם לתת לאיש כדרכיו וכפרי
מעלליו ירמיהו לב : יט

❀*Great in counsel, and mighty in performance; Your eyes are open upon all the ways of the sons of men. To give every one according to his ways, and according to the fruit of his doings.*

Jeremiah 32:19

Hundreds of philosophers and numerous cultures have relegated the Deity to the role of "watchmaker": He who sets things in motion and then stands back to observe the outcome. Understanding God's direct involvement not only in every facet of Creation but in every aspect of our day-to-day lives, means an appreciation of *Hashgacha* (Providence).

Divine Providence signifies God's guiding hand in every area of human endeavor. His Omnipresence bears no resemblance to pessimistic fatalism. It is actually a reflection of man's behavior for ד׳ צלך — "God's Providence follows like a shadow " (*Tehillim* 121:5). We cannot order up a destiny altered to our specifications, but we can fortify our requests through mitzva-adherence and acts of selflessness.

The Time of His Life

HERSHEL BAMBERGER maximizes time. A busy diamond wholesaler, he always prepares detailed schedules of his hectic daily routine, cramming as many appointments as possible into the crowded agenda. A credit, no doubt, to his German ancestry, he is never late for an appointment; in fact, Bamberger's reputation for punctuality is legendary.

Another thing Hershel never does is come early — it's anathema to his nature. Arriving early wastes precious time. He might arrive a minute (or less) before a meeting, a doctor's visit, a Gemara *shiur*, or a departing train — but never earlier than that. He prides himself on the precision of his calculations and good planning. He's got a whole repertoire of shortcuts and time-saving devices that even stunt men wouldn't risk in order to save a few seconds — like the time he caught a ride on a fire truck to beat midtown traffic.

There was, however, one exception — a fluke. He had simply miscalculated. It was back in the 'sixties when, after a whirlwind ten-day business trip to Detroit, Hershel found himself at Metropolitan Airport half an hour before departure time. Not only was he at a loss as to how to fill this half hour, never having had time to kill before, but he couldn't accept the fact that his careful planning had somehow gone awry.

After repeatedly checking the big clock on the wall of the airport lounge to verify this paradoxical reality, he finally became reconciled to the situation. He placed a few phone calls and then sat down with all the other passengers who had innocently complied with the airline check-in instructions. Alongside him sat an elderly gentleman with a long beard, black coat and oval hat which branded him anything but a native of the Midwest.

No sooner had Hershel taken his seat than his neighbor uttered an anxious yelp. The man slapped his forehead, grabbed his suitcase and leaped up from his chair. He shot a quick glance at the wall clock and began frantically scurrying from the information desk to the courtesy counter and back again.

HERSHEL RECOGNIZED the symptoms: obviously the man had left something important behind. He knew the feeling well for he too had occasionally forgotten precious items in the course of travel. Long ago he'd triplicated all of his keys and reduced his luggage to the barest essentials. Despite Hershel's list-making predilection, he had, just a few months earlier, forgotten a small pouch of gemstones in a client's shop and only become aware of the loss when he had displayed his merchandise to the next customer. Leaving something behind was the bane of the travelling salesman's existence — an occupational hazard.

"*Anshuldigt*," Hershel said, tapping his distraught companion on the shoulder, "my name is Bamberger. Have you misplaced something? Maybe I can help?"

"*Oiy*, have I misplaced something! I am a *meshulach* for a Jerusalem orphanage and — can you believe it? — I left my money satchel in the hotel room! What am I going to do?"

"I think you'd better retrieve the orphans' money — that *is* what you came here for, isn't it?"

"Of course, but the flight to New York leaves in half an hour and if I miss it, I won't make the connecting flight to *Eretz Yisrael!*"

Hershel no longer had any doubts as to why he had arrived at the airport early. "Follow me," he motioned to the *meshulach*, and together they darted out of the terminal.

WITH GLOBE-TROTTER aplomb, Hershel quickly hailed a taxi and instructed the driver to head downtown at top speed. The taxi driver leered in anticipation of the vicarious fulfillment of every cabbie's dream: "*Follow that car!*"

Fortunately, the late rush-hour traffic flowed in the opposite direction and they made the trip to the hotel in a matter of minutes. Hershel waited in the cab while the *meshulach* hurried into the lobby. For the entire six minutes it took until the man emerged with his satchel, Hershel kept a nervous eye on the second hand of his watch — willing it to slow down.

As much as he cared about helping his new-found friend, he couldn't afford to miss this last flight of the day to New York. His untimely arrival at the airport had allowed him the rare luxury of calling his wife to inform her that he would be taking the last flight after all, United #114. She took advantage of the call to let him in on the secret: The family had planned a festive celebration for the Bambergers' twenty-fifth anniversary that night. He just couldn't disappoint them all.

The driver was gunning the motor even before the car door slammed. Now, with only fourteen minutes to take-off, the race was on. The desperate rush to catch a flight was a familiar experience, indeed second nature for Hershel, but still his heart thumped with the extra boost of adrenalin. At every intersection a red light arrested their progress and each one took forever to turn green.

And the traffic! The stretch of highway to the airport had become a four-mile-long parking lot. Minutes ticked by much faster than the fare on the taximeter. The *meshulach* was on the brink of despair, but Hershel's mind was racing: If the driver approached from the airport's north side, near the cargo terminal, there was still a chance. It just might work...

A GAP APPEARED in the traffic and the cab surged forward. The sign for the airport turn-off loomed ahead and Hershel reviewed the plan a second time: He had once seen a private car drive out onto an airport runway — surely with special permission, but now was no time to concern themselves with technicalities.

Hershel wedged a fat cigar between his clenched teeth, leaned forward, and explained his idea to the driver. The cabbie looked in the rear-view mirror to check if his passenger was insane.

"Mister, iz yur head on tight? One wrong move an' we get jet-propelled into Lake Erie! Sheesh. I'm gettin' heart failure just thinkin' about it! Even if we pull it off, th' airport cops'll nab me, lift ma license, an' prob'ly impound ma cab!"

Hershel dropped a twenty-dollar bill on the seat next to the driver. "Yeah, well, like I wuz sayin', Andy Jackson always wuz one of ma favorite prezidents."

"If we catch our plane, you can add Ulysses S. Grant to

your collection." The cabbie spun the steering wheel and hit the accelerator, tearing across a traffic island to the exit ramp they had just passed.

HERSHEL, caught up in the excitement of it all, was beginning to enjoy himself. He sat on the edge of his seat scanning the tarmac ahead, chewing his cigar to shreds. The taxi weaved an obstacle course around cargo containers, and Hershel pounded his fist against the upholstery with boyish enthusiasm as they narrowly missed crashing into a forklift.

"Left, left!" he shouted when he saw the "Authorized Vehicles Only" sign. He wasn't really sure *which* way to head, since he had never seen the airport from that perspective, yet he spoke with the confidence born of experience. This antic was one of very few he hadn't tried before, but under the pressure of time, Hershel Bamberger was at his best. Besides, he was convinced that the merit of this mitzva would aid his navigation.

The cab swerved left. Hershel let out a whoop and smacked the driver with his hat as they took the turn on two wheels.

The dashboard clock told him there were only three minutes to take-off. United was known for its punctuality — a reputation Hershel now considered despicable. For the first time since leaving the hotel, he glanced over at the beneficiary of his *chessed,* and Hershel was suddenly jolted back to reality.

THE *MESHULACH* didn't seem to be holding up too well. Apparently, forgetting his money satchel had been more than enough excitement for the elderly Jerusalemite. His face was chalky and he was hyperventilating.

"Reb Bamberger," he gasped, "do you mind if we stop for a few seconds?" The tumultuous chase through Detroit Metropolitan Airport was sending his blood pressure soaring. It wasn't helping his ulcer much either, and he clutched his stomach tightly as yet another spasm gripped him.

"I thought you wanted to get back to *Eretz Yisrael?*"

"Yes, yes. But it isn't one of the mitzvos of *yeiharaig ve'al yaavor!*"

"Just leave it to me. I'll get us on that flight, please God!"

"I don't mean to sound ungrateful — *chalilah!*" he panted as he braced himself for another *zetz* into the front seat. "You've already been a tremendous..."

"There's th' runway lights," the cabbie broke in. "What am I suppose t' be lookin' for?"

"A United aircraft — pointed eastward."

"Reb Bamberger," the *meshulach* cried, unable to keep the note of desperation from his voice, "please let me off. You can have my ticket to *Eretz Yisrael,* but I'm not cut out for this. Another minute of this and you'll be able to send me back to the Holy Land as freight!"

"**M**ISTER," the cabbie bellowed over the din of roaring jet engines, "I ain't never been on this here side o' th' airport before. Ya think somethin's gonna take off or land 'bout now?" Hershel glanced at his watch. "Nah, we've got plenty of time."

Just then a monstrous image filled the rear-view mirror. "Ohh My GOSH! We shore's in trouble!!"

Hershel and the *meshulach* looked over their shoulders. "*Oiy vey's meer,*" the *meshulach* whimpered — and passed out.

Hershel nearly swallowed his cigar butt, but he quickly regained his composure.

"STEP ON IT!!"

"Ma foot's already through th' floorboards!"

"*Reb Yid,* wake up, wake up — we made it!" Hershel shouted, pointing his crumpled hat towards the gleaming United fuselage. "There it is!" he was jubilant with the rapture of victory. Nothing could compare with the heady feeling of accomplishment derived from catching a plane or a train at the very last second.

BUT HERSHEL'S JOY was premature. When the driver slammed on the brakes, the jet came into full view, and they watched in dismay as the truck-mounted gangway slowly backed off. The sealed cabin door seemed to deride them with smug satisfaction and all they had to show for their slap-bang escapade was a hefty taxi-fare. The three of them sat staring in silence and disbelief as United Airlines flight #114 took off — right on schedule.

Hershel was incredulous. He was so certain that his mitzva — helping out the hapless *meshulach* — would have gotten them on that plane. In far less deserving circumstances he had achieved far more miraculous feats.

Well, there was no point sitting on the runway bemoaning their fate. The driver made his way off the tarmac and headed for the passenger side of the departure terminal, now taking his time about it and giving the *meshulach*'s nerves a chance to unknot. They had nothing to look forward to but another night in "Motown."

Hershel was in no hurry to give his wife a call, knowing how disappointed she and everyone else would be. He made two reservations for the first New York-bound morning flight and arranged fare refunds, a process that kept him occupied for the better part of an hour.

Moping through a half-deserted lounge, he tried to absorb the events of the day. Where could he have gone wrong that his efforts should go so unrewarded?

He mulled this over again and again. Fishing some change out of his pocket, he bought two cups of tea from a vending machine and handed one to the *meshulach*. The man had gotten most of his color back and was in a talkative mood. He pulled out his brochures and receipt book and began describing his orphanage, and Hershel understood where the conversation was leading... But by this time his patience had run out, and he had yet to contend with his wife's exasperation.

U NABLE TO POSTPONE it any longer, he started dialling his home number, about ten minutes before he would have landed. How was he going to explain that "Stopwatch Bamberger" had missed the flight home — and the anniversary party!

The line was busy. Why was she talking on the phone with the house full of guests? he wondered. He dialled again. Still busy. Finally he heard it ring. It rang and rang — maybe twenty times — until a muffled voice answered: "Yes?"

"Shirley? It's me..."

"Heshy...? HESHY, HESHY!! Is that really you?"

"Yeah, yeah, I missed the flight. You see, I was..."

"Oh, thank God, thank God!!"

"What?"

"Heshy, don't you know? We just heard it on the radio — a terrible tragedy! We've been on the phone with the airline for over half an hour. Your flight, from Detroit... it, the plane — it crashed..."

Promise

MOSHE SHECHTER stood on the cold, deserted subway platform trembling like a man with a raging fever. An unprepossessing figure in black hat and dark suit, he would not normally have earned a second glance from any passersby, but the swollen, red-rimmed eyes behind his glasses and the anguished expression that contorted his mild features caused even the jaded Transit Authority policeman to wonder.

Moshe wasn't the average *avrech*. Even as early as elementary school he had shown a lot of promise. His *rebbes* had labeled him an *illui* and a *masmid,* designations which continued to be applied to the outstanding *talmid chacham* he had become. He gave a *shiur* in his *kollel* and his only desire in life was to study Torah and raise his children properly. Blessed with a wonderful wife, a beautiful family and an adequate livelihood, Moshe's world was complete. Until last week.

The patrolman continued to stare but Moshe was too preoccupied to notice. In his mind he sat at Channie's hospital bed looking down at his beautiful baby's angelic face, with its golden frame of tight curls, soft rosy cheeks, and shining blue eyes.

"They're wrong!" he told himself, but he was far too intelligent to indulge in self-deception. He had seen the X-rays himself and there was no mistake. Channie's wheezing and coughing, which had not responded to weeks of conventional treatment, had been finally diagnosed as an obstruction in her lung, a growth which was impairing her breathing and threatening her life.

T HE DOCTORS at Mount Sinai had delivered the news gently, but even with all their years of experience, could not hide their concern. They too were enchanted by little Channie's cherubic beauty and wished they could sound more optimistic.

Moshe would gladly have changed places with his child, plucked the vile growth from her chest and implanted it in his own, anything to spare her suffering. The surgery was yet to be scheduled and in the meantime he spent long days and sleepless nights at his daughter's bedside, anxiously watching her tiny chest rise and fall with each labored breath; uttering *Tehillim* with a fervor he'd never known before; playing silly games to entertain her; and holding back the tears. In a few weeks' time, the cold steel of the surgeon's scalpel would slice through his baby's flesh — the very thought was like a physical blow. And only afterward would the pathology lab determine the nature of the growth.

"If only it will be benign," Moshe kept saying to himself between the silent prayers he sobbed by heart.

A T MIDNIGHT he was unexpectedly relieved by another family member, who had to physically drag him away from Channie's bed. He stepped outside the hospital, so absorbed in his problem that he found it hard to relate to a city that continued to function as if nothing had happened.

Moshe tried to stop a taxi to take him home to Brooklyn, but the cabs sped by like yellow bullets. After twenty minutes without success, he walked towards the subway station, too groggy to remember that few sane people ride the subways at that hour.

Having to wait for a train that refused to come was more than Moshe's frazzled nerves could handle. His uncontrollable trembling increased until he imagined the entire platform was shaking beneath his feet, but it was only the first rumblings of the subway train, arriving at last.

As the train emerged from the dark tunnel and began its screeching halt that rose steadily in pitch before reaching its ear-splitting crescendo, Moshe's mouth opened involuntarily and released a long-suppressed scream.

THERE WERE only three other passengers in the car at that hour: two Blacks engrossed in changing the cassette on their enormous "Ghetto Blaster" at one end, and a reeking derelict at the other. To walk through to the next car would have required an effort beyond Moshe's present ability, so he chose a seat near the drunkard, distancing himself as much as possible from the bone-jarring noise that passed for music.

Even when the Black youths got off, Moshe couldn't muster the will to move from his seat. His eyes roamed unseeing over the graffiti-adorned subway posters, the color-coded route map, the vandalized fire extinguisher, and returned to his travelling companion.

The man was large-framed but his body was cadaverous, and he was obviously inebriated. In his hand was a brown paper bag that outlined a whiskey bottle. Razor lacerations crisscrossed his grey-tinged face and his deepset eyes, partially hidden below drooping lids, were moist and bloodshot. The stench that rose from his filthy clothes intensified as he raised the bottle to his lips and dribbled cheap rotgut down his shirt.

When the man's gaze fell upon him and remained there, Moshe became frightened. He felt faint; the tension of the past week, the fatigue coupled with fear made his stomach churn. He needed air. He turned to the grime-sealed windows, but he knew there was no hope of raising one without a crowbar. Suddenly the fetid smell grew stronger and closer. Moshe looked around and discovered that the drunkard had arisen from his seat and was standing over him, staring intently into his face.

MOSHE REALIZED he had to escape, perhaps try to ring the alarm bell or pull the emergency brake. But the man was too close, much too close. Moshe's blood froze in his veins and his heart pounded in his chest. The derelict raised his arm threateningly and heaved his empty bottle to the far side of the car, where it smashed against a bench. Moshe drew back from the drunk's foul breath and rotting teeth and tried to avoid his glance.

"You've grown a little bit but you're still the same skinny midget. Don't you recognize me, Professor?"

Moshe recoiled as if struck by a live wire. "Impossible," he stammered, "it's impossible! Binyamin Greenbaum?! How can it be? What has happened to you?"

Before Binyamin could answer, the conductor announced: "West Fourth Street."

"I, I have to change trains here," Moshe said, making his way towards the exit.

"Me, too," said Binyamin, not taking his eyes off Moshe. The doors snapped open and they disembarked.

MOSHE CROSSED OVER to the "Downtown" track and sat down on a bench to wait for the Brooklyn-bound IRT. To his astonishment, Binyamin took the seat alongside him. Moshe found it difficult to speak — what could he say? He couldn't believe that this repulsive individual had once been his classmate.

"Binyamin, how did this happen? How could you have fallen so far from our days in yeshiva?"

"The name is *Benjy*, Professor, Benjy *Green*. I'm not a young yeshiva *bochur* anymore, or hadn't you noticed? Look at me, Professor. Look at my hands." He lifted his trembling fingers to the light. "You see that? That's what 'junk' does to you."

"What? Drugs too?" Moshe exclaimed in a stricken voice.

"Yes, Professor. Soon I'll need another 'fix' and then I'll take your money just as fast as I'd swipe an old lady's handbag to get what I need."

"No! Benjy, you must let me help you!"

"It's too late. No one can help me now."

"Benjy, I beg of you. Go to a drug rehabilitation center. I'll come as soon as I can. As soon as..." he stopped abruptly, remembering why he couldn't come now. Tears welled up in his eyes and spilled down his cheeks. Benjy continued to stare at him blankly.

"Benjy," begged Moshe, "Binyamin, it is *I* who needs help — *your* help. I have faith in you. You must promise me that you will stop this, promise you will go to a rehabilitation center, please PROMISE! You must promise me, for perhaps in the merit of this my daughter will be spared..." He sobbed as he poured his heart out and told Binyamin about Channie's tumor and the operation she would need. But Benjy sank back into his drunken stupor and closed his ears to the sound.

A train was approaching. Moshe shook him and said, "Where can I get in touch with you?"

"Nowhere," he mumbled. "Well, I guess you could leave a message with my mother. I call her every couple of months. At our old house on Ninth Avenue." Moshe quickly scribbled his own phone number on a scrap of newspaper.

"Please, Binyamin, don't let me down. Call me — I beg of you!" Moshe hurried onto the train and looked through the windows at the huddled form of a ruined man.

THE COURTYARD of the Bnei Dovid Yeshiva in Boro Park was in a commotion. The students were conferring secretly in every corner of the school, for something terrible had happened: during recess one of the boys had sneaked into the teachers' room and had stolen Rabbi Yaggid's gradebook!

Yaggid knew that the culprit was from the eighth grade but he didn't know who; everyone had his suspicions. The principal was outraged, and assembled the class informing them in no uncertain terms that if they didn't tell him by the end of recess who had stolen the book, they could forget about the class trip to Washington D.C.

The students were torn: they subscribed to the unwritten code of mutual help which made snitching on a classmate a crime akin to manslaughter. But failure to report the felon meant jeopardizing the trip to Washington, the highlight of the school year. There was also the small matter of conscience, of telling the truth. What would they do?

MOSHE SHECHTER was always considered the best pupil of the class. Short in stature and with an unathletic physique, he was a serious boy who devoted himself to learning. Intent on his studies, he never joined the other boys for recess in the schoolyard, and today was no different. The events of the morning, therefore, were slow in penetrating his thoughts.

"Nu, Professor, what do you say?" came the taunting voice. Moshe lifted his head from his Gemara and saw the class low-lifes standing in front of his desk, led by the biggest bully of all — Binyamin Greenbaum. "Nu, Professor, say something already!" and they all burst out in raucous laughter.

Moshe turned red. He didn't know what they wanted from him. It wasn't the first time they had made fun of him, and for the life of him he couldn't figure out why they did. Greenbaum, their brawny leader, obviously had something against him.

Moshe thought about this a lot. What had he ever done to Greenbaum that he should pick on him so? He was half Binyamin's size, so he certainly couldn't be a threat to him.

Yet Greenbaum was always throwing a ball or a yo-yo at him and then pretending it was an accident. He even ambushed Moshe several times on the way home from school, sometimes to torment him, sometimes to beat him up.

But Moshe held his peace. He found different routes to walk home, which wasn't easy since they lived on the same street.

Bnei Dovid never had any *nachas* from Binyamin Greenbaum. He came from a broken home and barely was eligible for promotion from one grade to the next.

Everyone wanted to throw him out of the yeshiva, but the principal justified keeping him on by saying, "I cannot bear responsibility for this child's future if he is forced to leave grade school. Who knows what will become of him?"

THE BELL rang and recess was over. As usual Moshe didn't even bother answering Greenbaum, although he was now fairly certain who had stolen the gradebook.

The principal entered the classroom and fear gripped the pupils. "This is your last chance! I expect the person responsible to stand up like a man and confess." The room was charged with tension. Students turned to stare at Greenbaum who had his own gaze pointedly fixed on the ceiling. "They can all rot," he thought to himself, "I'm not telling..."

Five minutes passed and the principal bellowed: "Well?" The classroom was utterly silent. Suddenly, little Moshe Shechter, the teacher's pet, rose and said in a quavering voice: "I am the one." Jaws dropped in amazement and disbelief. The principal muttered, "It's impossible, impossible!" "I did it," Moshe repeated, his voice clearer now. "The others needn't suffer because of me and miss their trip. I am to blame."

That night Moshe walked home late. Only one streetlight was burning on the whole long block. Suddenly, he heard footsteps behind him — it was that awful bully Greenbaum. His heart thumped loudly. There was no one on the street to help him. Moshe started to walk quickly but the footsteps behind him quickened too. They got closer and closer. Moshe started to run but Greenbaum was faster and stronger.

"Professor," Binyamin called as he grabbed him by the shoulder and spun him around. Moshe was in a panic, too frightened to look up from the ground. Greenbaum forced his chin upward until their eyes met.

"Professor, I just wanted to say thank you," and he vanished into the darkness.

AT DAWN Benjy Green awoke. His whole body ached, and at first he couldn't remember where he was or how he had gotten there. And then memory flooded back in a rush. Benjy sat up on the bench. There were few people on the street and they all kept their distance. He knew why, but he couldn't care. He was used to it.

"So, the Professor thinks he can help me, huh?" Then Moshe's strange words came back to him: 'It is *I* who needs help... I have faith in you... my daughter will be spared.' The shaking started again.

"Alright!" he said aloud, deciding at last. "Where is that scrap of paper with his number?" He rummaged through his clothes. Where was it?

He dug nervously into every pocket, searching as if his life depended upon it. Deep down he knew that this phone number was his last chance, his only remaining link with the real, normal world he had abandoned so long ago.

"Oiy," he groaned in despair. "What have I come to since my days in Bnei Dovid? I'm nothing. An addict, a drunken bum, a sub-human creature people cross the street to avoid." He sobbed and rocked back and forth on the bench, arms crossed tightly against his stomach to quell the sickening tremors.

Suddenly he felt the scrap of paper. It seemed to galvanize him. He dug in his pockets frantically and found a solitary coin and began to search the lonely street for a phonebooth. He dialled with quivering fingers, not even waiting to hear the voice at the other end. Moshe was just leaving for the hospital when the phone rang.

"Professor? This is Benjy. I..." His voice faltered.

"Yes, my friend?" Moshe urged.

'Friend,' thought Benjy. When was the last time someone had called him 'friend?'

"I'm taking your advice and going to a drug center. I tried once before, but it was murder, believe me, and I swore I'd never go back. This time I'm doing it for your little girl." Benjy hung up.

MOSHE COULDN'T believe his ears. Binyamin Greenbaum had sunk to the lowest depths of depravity, yet he was willing to admit himself to a rehabilitation center for Channie's sake, a little girl he had never even met. But where was he? Why did he hang up? Moshe had no time to do anything about it — he had to get to the hospital.

After Channie fell asleep, Moshe slipped out of the room and began an exhaustive telephone search to locate Benjy. He spent fruitless hours talking to operators and thumbing through all the boroughs' directories. He was at his wits' end.

At last a clerk from the City Commission on Drug Rehabilitation remembered something: "Wait a minute," she said, "there is one more place — the Waverly Center. They take only the most critical cases there — the 'goners.'" Moshe called and quickly verified that Benjy had been admitted that morning. He grabbed a taxi to the Center.

Moshe introduced himself as a friend of Green's and said that he was prepared to do anything he could to help. But the counselors were very cautious. "This is a most severe case. He's hopelessly addicted. Even if he can make it here, there's no guarantee he'll make it on the outside. There are serious complications, too. Try calling in about a week..."

When Moshe called again he asked if he could come over. "There's no point in coming now," the attendant advised. "You can't imagine what he's going through and he still hasn't gotten over the worst. The man is in really bad shape. But he's aware of your involvement — and that's what's keeping him going. Don't come now, it's too early. He's got to do this on his own — no one else can do it for him."

A few days later, Channie underwent surgery. The Shechters were on tenterhooks waiting for word from the doctor. They prayed, and cried, and waited. At last the surgeon emerged from the operating room with a smile on his face and the magic words on his lips: "It was benign. She's going to be alright."

Moshe phoned the Waverly Center and this time a doctor came on the line. "Are you next of kin?" he asked.

"No," Moshe replied, "just a friend."

"In that case, you must be the 'Professor.' He says he owes his life to you. But I have to tell you, Benjy is a very sick man. There's extensive liver damage and his heart's not too strong either. Can't say how long he's got — even if he does kick his drug habit." Moshe was stunned.

"When can I visit him?" The doctor suggested he wait a little longer and assured Moshe he would convey his message to Green.

F IVE WEEKS after he was admitted to the Center, Benjy was able to leave for a few hours by himself. He remembered with a smile the phone conversation he'd had the night before: the Professor had related that Channie was recuperating rapidly and thanked Benjy — profusely! — for the role he had played in her recovery. Benjy promised to visit after a stop at his mother's. It would be his first real 'social call' since — he couldn't remember when.

It was bitter cold outside and winds gusted all around him in a whir. Benjy took several deep breaths of fresh air before descending the stairs to the subway. As he passed a vending machine he caught sight of his reflection in the streaked mirror. He almost didn't recognize himself. He not only felt like a new man, he looked like one.

The Center had given him fresh clothes and he had

shaved carefully and combed his newly-trimmed hair. His mother would be pleased, he thought, and then he started to shiver with apprehension at this first contact with humanity outside the Center. He needed a drink. He bought a candybar instead and boarded the waiting train.

At one of the stations, a woman got on and sat on the bench facing his. She opened her pocketbook, removed her wallet to check the contents, and replaced it. This commonplace act triggered a reflex in Benjy's brain that made him forget where he was coming from and where he was headed. "One quick snatch and it's mine," he thought.

The train moved on and the woman, along with many of the passengers, dozed off. She released her grip on the purse in her lap; Benjy waited impatiently for the right moment.

J UST THEN the lights went out and the darkened train came to a halt. "A blackout," one passenger sighed. "Who knows how long we'll be stuck here."

Benjy moved cautiously. Soon the purse would be his and no one would be the wiser. But the shaking in his hands began to act up again; they refused to cooperate. "It'll pass in a second," he told himself, and then he heard something strange that made his entire body quake.

"Hey! What's that noise? Who's crying?" But the crying he heard came from within his soul. "What's the matter with me?" He was drenched with sweat and the sound of weeping grew louder. "It's not me," he gasped, "it's *to* me! It's the Professor!"

"You promised me... In your merit she was saved... you promised me you wouldn't steal... you promised to change... you promised me..."

BENJY'S HEAD SPUN; he felt faint. He leaned back against the bench and tried to regain control of himself. "Get out of here, Professor!" he screamed in his heart. "Leave me alone. It's hard! It's so hard — I can't promise! The money's right here. I need it! No..."

The electricity in the train returned. The second it flickered on Benjy saw a pickpocket's nimble fingers dive into the lady's purse and remove her wallet. The blood rushed to his head. He hurled himself at the thief and shouted:

"Don't take it! I promised him, do you hear me? If *I* didn't steal it, neither will you! I promised. I kept my word!"

But the mugger wasn't impressed with the ravings of a madman. He threw a punch at Benjy's face, jabbed an elbow into his ribs, and Benjy dropped to the floor. His weakened heart in a wasted body couldn't withstand the injury.

MOSHE WAITED and waited for Benjy. After three hours of tense anxiety, he called the Waverly and was told only that Benjy Green had left in the morning headed for "the Professor."

By mid-afternoon Moshe could contain his fears no longer. Could Benjy still be at his mother's? He hurried out and headed for the address on Ninth Avenue.

AT THE STEPS of the brownstone, a group of people had gathered; the scene made Moshe's heart skip a beat. "Did something happen?" he asked with trepidation. "The poor woman," responded a neighbor, "they just told her that her son was killed." Another man joined in: "And did you hear what the police say? He was trying to save a lady from a mugger!"

"What?!" Moshe exclaimed incredulously. "But he was

so weak!" Everyone turned towards him wondering how he was involved. "That's exactly what they said," the neighbor continued. "As soon as the lights went back on in the train he jumped like a lunatic at the other guy and yelled: 'Don't steal! I didn't steal. I promised!' Maybe you know what he was talking about, huh, Mister?"

A few months after Channie's operation the Shechters had a son. Despite all their questioning, no one could pry out of Moshe his reason for giving the baby a name foreign to the family: Binyamin Chaim.

Moshe would only say: "I am paying back a debt, for a promise that was kept."

Free Will Meets Divine Providence

A lovely young woman sat at the far end of the bench at the #39 bus stop. She wore no makeup over her delicate features, and her attire was simple and modest, yet she emanated the kind of beauty that comes from within. Mordechai smiled to himself thinking that just half a year ago, a religious girl like this would never have caught his eye. Why, he wouldn't even have been in a religious neighborhood then, at least not willingly. But that is really the essence of this story, an object lesson in the age-old issue of *Hashgacha Pratis* and *Bechira Chofshis*, or as the philosophers like to call it: Providence vs. Free Will.

Three months before, Mordechai was still Martin, Martin Harris: self-styled atheist, Princeton, Class of '79, Harvard Graduate School, Class of '83 — a post-graduate iconoclast and full-time skeptic. His reasons for visiting Israel in the summer of '82 are a bit hazy, but one could say that Napoleon sent him. "A man cannot become an atheist merely by wishing it," wrote Monsieur Bonaparte, a thought which probably originated with the tale of *Berel the Apikores*. Martin had decided to prove the Emperor wrong. Thus, Martin's trip had nothing to do with searching for his roots, except, perhaps, to dig them up and spray them with weed-killer.

I N KEEPING WITH his myth-debunking image, Martin was determined not to set foot in Jerusalem, declaring it a 'decadent city.' On a purely intellectual level, he considered Jerusalem the ultimate symbol of an irrational, reactionary faith, but his need to keep his distance was strictly emotional. Jerusalem meant a confrontation — doing battle with a much-challenged, long-despised foe. Deep down inside, Martin wanted to avoid this final confrontation because he could not be sure of the outcome.

He had long since learned that cold rational arguments are powerless in the face of religious fervor. On more than one occasion he had seen intelligent friends abandon reason for the emotional lure of faith. At both his Ivy League schools he'd met Jewish boys who had become observant through initially innocuous visits to Jerusalem and the Western Wall — visits which led to entry into a '*baal teshuva*' yeshiva. They emerged unrecognizable, as though they had been not just brainwashed but spun-dry and hung on the line together with their fringed white prayer shawls.

He wouldn't allow himself to get sucked in and the best way to beat temptation, he theorized, was to avoid it. But then again, he countered mentally, such reasoning was specious. Those who were ensnared by Judaism were weak-kneed, unstable people who were searching for 'something' in the first place. And he, being of sound mind and balanced reason, had nothing to fear. Surely the infamous Western Wall, the bear-trap that claimed so many unsuspecting spirituality-seekers as its victims, would never claim Martin Harris. If four years of Sunday School, a set of obtrusive grandparents, and scores of friends and colleagues could not influence his outlook, neither could a pile of old stones. And yet he avoided the city.

S O MUCH for Free Will; the rest is Providence. One torrid July afternoon, Martin waited nearly two hours for a hitch from Ein Gedi to Tiberias. The one car that finally stopped to offer him a ride, was headed for... Jerusalem. He really didn't have much of a choice. In an hour the sun would have set and the road would be a long lonely stretch after dark. He was parched and almost prostrate from the heat after his lengthy wait. He felt like a poached egg. Still he found it hard to accept the ride and contemplated his options.

"Nu?" the driver queried impatiently. Martin realized that this wasn't the time to subject his sun-baked cerebrum to polemics, so he tossed his backpack through the open rear window and sat down next to the driver.

"What's the matter?" asked the driver. "You were expecting a stretch-limo to take you to Tel Aviv?"

"No, no, I'm sorry. I'm really very grateful for the lift. It's just that I wasn't thinking of heading for Jerusalem..."

"What's wrong with Jerusalem? You're Jewish, aren't you?"

"Jewish? Well, my parents are."

"Then what are you, a biological anomaly?"

"I just don't believe in that whole religion business."

"What does that have to do with Jerusalem?"

"Jerusalem is where it's all at. You know, yeshivas, synagogues, the Western Wall — the works."

"Listen, I'm not religious myself. But I'm not compulsive

either. Don't fight it! Go to Jerusalem and pay your respects to the Wall, just like every other tourist — and Jew!"

Martin's brain ached. What ever happened to Free Will? It was as if the matter had been taken out of his hands. He realized with a jolt that he would even be obliged to spend the night in Jerusalem for by the time they arrived there, he would be too tired to make the trip north to Tiberias. The driver let him off near the Damascus Gate to the Old City, an area teeming with youth hostels.

TO MARTIN'S RELIEF, the East Jerusalem locale and the residents in the Damascus Gate vicinity were anything but Jewish. In fact, from the look of things, he would have thought he was in Jordan.

He entered the huge gate and stopped at the first shop to buy a drink and get his bearings. "Can you tell me where I can find a hostel?" he asked the proprietor.

"Sure, sure. Just follow the signs to the Wall."

Martin nearly choked on his Coke. He looked up and saw arrow signs posted every few feet pointing 'To The Western Wall.' Here he was, in East Jerusalem, strolling innocently down the Via Dolorosa — headed for the Western Wall. "I guess there's no avoiding my 'Appointment in Samara,' " Martin muttered to himself as he slung his backpack over his shoulder. "*Que sera, sera...*"

HE TRUDGED DOWN the strange-smelling, narrow, winding passageways. Suddenly, the open courtyard in front of the Wailing Wall greeted him like a serene haven after the bedlam of the Arab *shuk*. Not that he felt any more at home with the people milling about the Wall: There were devoutly religious ladies with kerchiefs pulled tightly around their heads, chassidim talking and reciting Psalms, soldiers praying with Uzis tucked under their arms, elderly men and women jangling charity collection boxes and dozens of worshipers swaying to rhythms only they could hear.

"Such a big deal over these rocks!" Martin thought. "A wall is a wall. In Harvard Yard there are plenty of walls like this — with smaller bricks and covered with ivy, naturally." He moved closer and found the stones dotted with little slips of paper the faithful had crammed into the crevices. These slips only heightened his incredulous scorn. "What are they, inter-office memos to the Boss?" he snickered to himself.

"God," called Martin, commencing his atheistic prayer, "if that is in fact Your name, and You do indeed exist, show me a sign — some indication that You are here, or there — or anywhere..."

NO SOONER had these words crossed his lips than he felt a tap on his shoulder. "Pardon me, but maybe you would care to attend an interesting lecture in a yeshiva nearby, or perhaps you need a place to stay overnight?" The 'master of serendipity,' otherwise known as Rabbi Meir Shuster, struck again.

Martin's mind reeled like a rider slipping off a speeding roller coaster. His sinewy self-reliance crumbled. "ALRIGHT, O.K.!!" he shouted back.

Even Meir Shuster, who has been guiding lost souls to *baal teshuva* institutions every day of the year, rain or shine, for more than a decade, had never witnessed such a reaction. Fearing another eruption, Shuster quickly whisked Martin off to Aish HaTorah, a (*baal teshuva*) yeshiva located in the Jewish Quarter of the Old City. "Go easy with this one," Rabbi Shuster whispered uncharacteristically to the yeshiva personnel assigned to process newcomers.

MARTIN'S STRIDENT skepticism was met with compassion and fatherly firmness. His challenges and arguments brought unshakeable responses. After three weeks in yeshiva, his barriers began to fall, and he jockeyed between quasifunk and unwavering fealty. He gradually allowed his mind to open to new levels of rational thought and discovered the roots he had sought to destroy. Within a short time, he had made the long and arduous journey toward religious commitment. He postponed his trip home, and embarked upon the road leading to observance.

Three months later, Martin/Mordechai, like so many others who enter Aish HaTorah and similar yeshivos, was a new person, or at least a richer, more complete one. Not only had his commitments changed but so had his values. He began to look forward to marriage, raising a family and living as his forebears had lived.

Before carrying out his new plans, however, he had to return to Boston to complete his thesis. He would surely be taking back with him a lot more than just a collection of memories of 'My Trip to Israel.'

TAKING LEAVE OF some of his new-found friends in a religious Jerusalem neighborhood was something Mordechai did of his own Free Will. But the presence of the lovely girl at the bus stop was surely Divinely-planned. Later that evening, the very same girl stood on line ahead of him at the El Al luggage check-in. Could it have been random coincidence that placed her in the seat next to his on the flight to Boston?

With admirable restraint, they exchanged only a few casual words during the entire flight. Mordechai had already had one amazing bout with Divine Providence at the Wall and felt he shouldn't push his luck. "If she's really for me," he thought, remembering something he'd learned in yeshiva, "I'll meet up with her again."

And he did. Mordechai's first Shabbos in Boston at the Young Israel of Brookline, found his travelmate on the other side of the *mechitza*.

THE FOLLOWING WINTER, the Harrises — Mr. and Mrs. — returned to Jerusalem so that Mordechai could enter *kollel* and begin a life where *Hashgacha Pratis* and *Bechira Chofshis* work in concert to create their own unique Jewish symphony.

3

on Devotion

והביאותים אל הר קדשי
ושמחתים בבית תפלתי עולֹתיהם
וזבחיהם לרצון על מזבחי כי ביתי
בית־תפלה יקרא לכל העמים

ישעיה נו : ז

And I will bring them to My holy mountain, and make them joyful in My house of prayer. Their burnt offerings and their sacrifices shall be acceptable upon my altar — for My house shall be called a house of prayer for all peoples.

Isaiah 56:7

Prayer in Judaism is an open line of communication to the Almighty, giving finite man limitless access to his Infinite Creator. The only prerequisite for guaranteeing that his message will be heard is *kavana* — "devotion." Prayer without devotion, writes the *Chovos HaLevavos*, is like "a body without a soul, a shell without a kernel."

A standardized liturgical style helps to organize and focus our thoughts and feelings. In order to enhance our devotion, a specific venue is required. The familiarity of the surroundings stimulates thought processes that imbue our silent supplications with meaning. Some shuls, although devoid of the many conventional synagogue trappings, are uniquely suitable for a spiritual rendezvous.

Forecast:
Light Showers
And Heavy Prayers

RAIN. In New York it comes down in sheets whipped with urgent winds that buffet hapless pedestrians from street corner to lamp-post. Umbrellas — useless encumbrances when forced inside-out by a diabolical gust — offer little protection against the tidal waves which crest without warning from beneath the wheels of vengeful taxis.

In Vienna rain carries with it a chill that penetrates the thickest mittens and sturdiest boots. Live trolley sparks are instantly snuffed out and die sizzling on their tracks. Raindrops beat staccato rhythms on the tin roofs of tram cars, a relentless cacophony that defeats all but the most valiant efforts at conversation.

In London the rain falls perpetually, day after dreary day, until the cloud-laden sky has wrung itself out. Ubiquitous "brollies" at last get pressed into service, no longer mere props. And the fog, a tangible shroud over the metropolis, conceals beneath its folds the pinched, tight-lipped British countenances which will have to relearn the art of smiling when winter ends.

NOT SO in Tel Aviv. In this sun-kissed coastal city where the mercury rarely falls below freezing, a winter rainstorm is hardly more than a spring shower, just enough for rose petals to moisten their parched lips. At most, half the population owns a raincoat; the other half could never decide whether to wear one: "Surely it will clear up by mid-morning..."

Newspaper sales increase on rainy days. *Yediot* is conveniently proportioned for tenting over bare heads or costly hats; *Haaretz*, however, is unwieldy. In a country noted for its pragmatism, a temporary shelter for temporary inclemency could be a national slogan, readily applicable to other areas.

Those who spurn the newspaper solution are not above yanking up a jacket collar to form a tolerable hairdo-protector. A few sophisticates wrestle with willful folding umbrellas but often as not by the time these are unfurled, the crisis has passed.

The majority of Tel Avivians turn their tanned faces skyward to welcome the rain, some with hope that the long-awaited precipitation will precipitate a drop in produce prices; others with gratitude to God for His bountiful blessing.

Rain in Tel Aviv doesn't empty the streets; on Allenby Street, it's "business as usual." Moped and scooter riders weave through heavy traffic with damp windbreakers but undampened chutzpah. A herd of buses growls up and down the boulevard while bicyclists follow suit with their heads tilted down, to keep the rain, as it were, out of their eyes.

Outdoor cafe regulars, some thoroughly drenched, just become more firmly entrenched. And nothing deters Allenby's cadre of veteran window-shoppers. State-of-the-art windowdressing lures even the diehard penny-pincher with offers of "Export Quality," "Newest Imports," "No Inflation Here," and "Last Week's Dollar Rate Accepted." The signs and attractions displayed in the windows are a sociological index of the Israeli mentality.

The sidewalks are so teeming with humanity, that a lone raindrop can scarcely find a decent spot to land. During business hours Rechov Allenby is waterproof.

E VEN THE TOURISTS refuse to succumb. Guidebooks in hand and cameras slung over weary shoulders, they wend their way along Allenby in search of something worthy of recording for posterity. They stop before an inspiring edifice, indistinguishable from the banking establishments with which it rubs elbows.

This, the guidebook claims, is the Great Synagogue of Tel Aviv, a superb example of indigenous Israeli architecture. It is surrounded by imposing though somewhat graceless pillars, the sole purpose of which — beyond demonstrating the versatility of poured concrete — is to provide an elegant perch for endemic Israeli pigeons.

The tourists naively rattle the doorhandle. "Naively" because, as any Tel Avivian knows, the Great Synagogue is, for all practical purposes, no more than a monument to the lack of foresight of demographic planners. Optimistically erected a mere half-century ago, it was intended as a central house of worship for the burgeoning town.

By the time the building was finally completed (on Tel Aviv's bar mitzva), the city had begun to expand northward, throwing residential districts miles away and obviating the Great Synagogue's *raison d'être*. With the exception of a wedding or an organized tour, it is only on rare occasions that the massive doors are flung open to admit a visiting VIP for a peek at its inner glories.

Let it not be said that the building has no intrinsic value whatsoever: if not for the existence of the Great Synagogue, there would be no Great Synagogue basement; and if not for the Great Synagogue basement, there would be no *Mincha Minyan;* and if not for the *Mincha Minyan,* this would be no story. *Dayeinu.*

ACCESS TO the Great Synagogue basement is via a route heretofore known only to a privileged few. The well-concealed, unmarked entrance is through the adjoining alley and down the steps — bear right under the ventilation duct. Exposed fluorescent strip-lighting and floors and walls of — yes — poured concrete enhance the purely functional decor of this *Mikdash Me'at* (emphasis on the "*me'at*"). It is so dingy and run-down that its juxtaposition to the Great Synagogue is a lesson in oxymoronics.

But to the faithful — some thirty or more local bank clerks, insurance agents, store owners, office managers, and even a Gerrer chassid who works at Alter's book store on Montefiore Street — the basement is a shul. They come seeking not a refuge from the rain (for they embark on this pilgrimage daily), but a haven from the rat race.

Elderly European survivors of Nazi terrors and tyrannies who rebuilt shattered lives on these Mediterranean shores; wealthy Persian Johnny-come-lately's who escaped the Ayatollah's maniacal fanaticism with only a few priceless carpets on their backs; unlettered

Moroccans who had to claw their way to a respectable position in Israeli society; Western immigrants, the entrepreneurs who gave new meaning to the phrase "Anglo-Saxon" — all gather in the Great Synagogue basement with a unity of purpose that obliterates any superficial differences.

THE BUZZING of a single fly echoes like a swarm of bees in this empty chamber. It is five minutes to three and the bare fluorescents and concrete walls have only the fly for company. At three o'clock, the front of the shul is packed, with hardly room to take three stiff backward steps for *Shemoneh Esrei*.

For the men of the *Mincha Minyan,* prayer is a serious business. They all arrive on time because they have little of that precious commodity to spare. Rain does not reduce their number. A pile of wet newspapers crumpled near the door and faint clouds of steam rising from damp grey work smocks are the only testimony to the inclement weather.

Time-wasting chitchat is frowned upon. Such chatter may abound in the offices and shops — but not here. Greetings are cut off in mid-phrase with one "clop" from the *chazzan,* and "*Ashrei yoshvei veisecha*" never sounded so sweet.

Those three words banish the cares and woes of eking out a livelihood, of dental bills and income taxes and municipal rates.

The man examining inventory slips stuffs them and his half-rim glasses into his pocket. He stretches his hands heavenward as he did as a boy in Cracow. Just two generations earlier he was one of the thousands who flooded Cracow's cobbled alleys on the way to the shtiebel *for Mincha. "Ashrei yoshvei veisecha" said in a grimy Allenby retreat brings him back to the world of Mishnayos and Chok between Mincha and Maariv, to his cheder and dear parents who are no more...*

FOR A FEW carefully scheduled minutes in a hectic workday every man present can close his eyes and be transported to a long-ago, far-away "home" that never dims in his memory: the concrete walls become draped with silken tapestries; the harsh fluorescents turn into crystal chandeliers; the unadorned *aron kodesh* is hand-carved wood, polished lovingly to a deep, rich gloss. "Happy are those who dwell in Your house" — the worshipers recite the *Mincha* service mostly by heart and each in his own *nusach*, but their voices ascend as one clear note.

Perhaps, for just a few minutes in a hectic workday, Rechov Allenby pauses to provide a little *nachas* to the Almighty. This unpretentious *mikdash me'at* shines above its decadent surroundings and the *tefillos* rise like a *rei'ach nicho'ach*.

At three-fourteen the *Kaddish* is chanted in ten or more distinct dialects. At three-fifteen the basement of the Great Synagogue is an empty chamber once more.

ONE MAN REMAINS, reciting *Tehillim* and savoring the aura of spirituality that lingers on in a room far more inspiring than the cavernous hall above, and far more blessed than the street outside. After a minute, he sighs, stoops to retrieve his paper umbrella, and dashes across the rain-dappled street, comforted by the thought that what brought him here today will draw him back again.

All The Shul's Men

When it comes to shuls, Jews seem to have an "Edifice Complex," a condition characterized by the proliferation of monumental synagogue structures in Jewish communities the world over. Even where *minyanim* gather in less grandiose houses of worship, the sums of money they expend for beautification and refurbishing are staggering. Who can say what suppressed urges are sublimated thereby, or deep-seated needs fulfilled, or sins expiated? The congregants of the Ohr Yaakov shul are notably free of this (particular) neurosis.

Meah Shearim/Beis Yisrael was among the first neighborhoods established outside the Old City walls, in the late nineteenth century. The building which houses the Ohr Yaakov shul in Beis Yisrael dates from that period, and from the look of things, nothing has been disturbed there since. The shul's only concession to the March of Time was the substitution of its defunct gas lamps with fluorescent lighting, a renovation carried out at least one, if not two generations ago. The burnt-out bulbs have not (yet) been replaced.

Around the same time, all the tables, benches, walls and *shtenders* received a coat of what must have been grey paint. The only evidence of this ambitious undertaking are a few surviving scabs of enamel. It is through their efforts alone that two of the *shtenders* remain erect; all the others have been converted into "legless wonders" — Portable *Shtender*/Laptrays.

EARTHQUAKES, wars and countless shuffling feet have reduced the marble floor tiles to a wild mosaic of crevices, cracks and fissures. These serve as repositories for coins, stamps, lint and other pocket debris, some dating back to the Mandate.

The raised central *bima,* accessible via staircases on either side (*watch your step!*) is surrounded by an ornamental iron railing. It's impossible to estimate the number of hats and coats that have hung thereon, or, for that matter, the age of the "towel" which ornaments it. But it's a snap to guess the number of times the "towel" has been laundered... This multi-functional rag, when not being used to (sort of) dry the *kohein*'s hands before *duchening,* has been known to dust off seats and sop up leaks, with equal effectiveness.

The walls are plastered with faded, dog-eared notices such as: "Lost — watch. Please return" (no signature) or "Joyous *kiddush* this Shabbos" (no date). In any other environment these signs would be incomprehensible, or, worse, laughable. In the Ohr Yaakov shul, they neither require elaboration nor elicit comment.

Although the shul is essentially a large, square room, unlike most squares, it has considerably more than four corners. Each "corner" delineates the private territory of one of the members of the *Vasikin* (sunrise) *minyan.*

LAIBEL the hardware store owner looks, appropriately enough, as though he eats nails for breakfast. He occupies the first of these domains. Tall and brawny, and with a voice that would shake steel-reinforced concrete foundations, Laibel could double as bodyguard for Attila the Hun.

But beneath this gruff exterior beats the heart of a pussycat, and one with a rollicking sense of humor, to boot. He collects jokes like some people collect rare coins. When he peeks over his half-moon glasses with that twinkle in his eye, it means he's about to unleash a roaring guffaw loud enough to make the *sefer Torah* bells ring from the vibrations.

Anshel is the steady *baal tefilla*, a man blessed with a mellifluent, resonant voice. It seems his vocal chords are capable of producing only music: when Anshel talks, he sings; when Anshel laughs, he sings; even when Anshel thinks, he sings. Conversations are the lyrics for his original melodies:

TO SAY THAT Alter Fleischfoos is a "ham" doesn't do justice to his prodigious theatrical abilities. All the shul is his stage. His hands — a study in perpetual motion — vividly express every word he prays. It goes without saying that he has a limitless repertoire of wails, moans, groans, and "*vey, veys.*" Alter is the only man who can sigh with sixteen different inflections. In addition to his *davening* antics, he has several "special" routines, plus a few encores thrown in for good measure.

For example, he collects *tzedaka* in the middle of *davening*. Collecting *tzedaka* is basically a common, innocuous activity; Alter Fleischfoos has turned it into a Broadway production:

(ACT I, Scene 1) Alter slams down a topless-coffee-can/*pushka* on the bench in front of the person he wishes to solicit, scattering coins all over the room. Laibel's jaw goes slack in an expression that means: "Here comes that Fleischfoos again!"

(Scene 2) Alter pantomimes (out loud) the recipients' dire financial straits, or points to the flaking ceiling and filthy floor which desperately require maintenance.

(Scene 3) Laibel, who knows how to handle Fleischfoos, drops a *tefillin baitel* into the can. Alter rolls his *eyes* and stamps his foot.

(ACT II, Scene 1) Laibel responds in kind. A gesticulation match ensues, lasting for several minutes.

(FINALE) Fleischfoos moves on, seeking a more sympathetic audience.

(CURTAIN)

KRECHTZMAN IS Ohr Yaakov's enigma. Wrapped securely in a yellowed *tallis*, he rarely casts his beady eyes on the goings-on. He owns a broom closet-sized shop in Meah Shearim for old *sefarim* of little interest. The singular lack of commerce might lead one to suspect that the shop is a front for some other activity as mysterious as its proprietor.

What renders Krechtzman unique is that he sticks to his corner. The others clock a lot of mileage before *Shacharis* is over: fifteen circuits, six transverse crossings, and one peripheral survey is considered about average. But Krechtzman is silently oblivious to all this peregrination. He just rocks — back and forth, back and forth, like a metronome, only with greater precision. It is his totally conventional behavior that makes him seem so thoroughly out of place.

One of the corners in the center of the *Mizrach* wall belongs to a director of the Badatz* Kashrus Division. This adds considerably to the traffic flow in the shul since the corner serves as a local branch of his office. A constant stream of outsiders bring their kashrus-related *shailos* to Ohr Yaakov, occasionally with the product in question still squawking. The birds discover to their relief that this director deals only with processed edibles.

One particular congregant seems to shun any form of public exposure — the late-blooming *"bochur."* A single fellow in his upper thirties, with sufficient idiosyncrasies to match his years, he probably selected this early *minyan* so that no one would notice his absence of *tallis*. It's conceivable, however, in this context, that he is actually married... and not wearing a *tallis* is one of his idiosyncrasies. Regardless, his secret is safe at Ohr Yaakov.

T HESE MEN ARE the Ohr Yaakov shul. No Judeo-American edifice could house them. Blazing chandeliers would dim alongside the brilliance of their glowing personalities; decorative acoustic ceilings couldn't muffle their chorus of meaningful prayer. But throngs of worshipers and velvet upholstered benches would stifle their uninhibited spontaneity: arms can't flail in a crowd and only a "legless wonder" could withstand the kinds of beatings Fleischfoos & Co. administer.

Angels, the Talmud says, pray at sunrise. Each morning, these men, in their own inimitable way, make a valiant effort to emulate their celestial counterparts. Not just with their words, but with their body and soul.

* *Beis Din Tzedek,* an organization which protects and promotes religious interests.

The Other Synagogue

HE MAGNIFICENT Chagall windows at Hadassah Hospital's synagogue are the highlight of many an organized tour to the Holy Land. If Hadassah had a dollar for every "spiritual leader" who enjoined his flock to "bow our heads and pray" beneath those awesome stained glass creations, the hospital could probably afford to sponsor several Hadassah chapters abroad.

"Awesome," however, is a far cry from "awe-inspiring." Even a tourist must find it difficult to conjure up a passable level of *kavana* from inside a museum, or to read the fine print in his "travelling siddur" with dozens of dazzling flash cubes bursting in twelve directions. Well, it's the experience that counts...

But for those who already own a permaplaqued version of the Chagallian masterpieces and seek an experience of a different sort, there is an alternative: the "other" Hadassah Synagogue. It's not generally included in tour itineraries and it's somewhat less grand than the famous one, but it is no less impressive — and far more *kavana*-conducive.

This shul — actually no more than a small room off a main corridor of the hospital — has no wall-to-wall carpeting, no fancy wooden pews, no hand-carved *aron kodesh*... and no endowment fund for its maintenance. Its spartan decor, in fact, is comprised of whatever could be scavenged or salvaged from the hospital rubbish heap or expropriated from the wards.

The benches were "donated" by one of the clinics; the *mechitza,* in its previous incarnation, was a portable privacy screen; a three-legged reception desk received a prosthetic limb and a starched white sheet and became the *shulchan*; an obsolete medicine cabinet serves as a bookcase for *siddurim* and *chumashim*. In short, the shul is totally compatible with its antiseptic environment and ideally suited for its purpose: this is a place for *davening* — not photographing.

ROSH HASHANAH is one of the best times to visit. There's no need to reserve seats in advance or pay outrageous fees for the privilege of praying. Patients from all the wards — the ambulatories and the not-so-ambulatories — find their way here. Some come with walkers, others with trailing I.V. poles or whatever contraption they happen to be hooked up to. Neither canes nor crutches nor casts can keep them away on Judgment Day.

In this shul it isn't the mellow voice of the *chazzan* or the rabbi's well-rehearsed *teshuva* sermon that evokes *kavana* — but the congregation itself. The sight of these tortured, twisted bodies, the patched and plastered and bruised faces, suffices to raise *kavana* levels to previously unexplored heights. Awash in this sea of misery, even the iciest soul must melt.

BUT THE *davening* is not without its lighter moments. Like any *shtiebel*, this one has its share of "characters." Goldberg is a prime example. He was admitted last *Pesach*, which entitles him to a certain status by virtue of his fine attendance record. His brother-in-law's nephew is an orderly — that's how he gets his bed wheeled in, monitors and all.

There's always one wise guy who raids the laundry on *erev Yom Tov* and brings a pile of fresh white doctors' coats. That way there are plenty of *kittels* to go around. And diapers from the nursery — mustn't forget the ladies. Even the less observant ones wouldn't attend Rosh Hashanah services without a kerchief.

Of necessity, the services are brief: the congregants' stamina is understandably limited. At eleven o'clock, a nurse is bound to show up from one of the wards, pushing a laden medicine trolley. The patients look up expectantly, as if she's handing out awards instead of castor oil and coumadine.

Once, a fellow in the second row took advantage of a break in the services to whip a stethescope out of his pocket and examine the congregant on his left — he didn't like the sound of the man's breathing. It's not hard to tell the doctors from the patients: the doctors don't have baggy striped pajamas sticking out the bottom of their *kittels*.

Another time there was a "Code Blue" right in the middle of *shofar*-blowing and they had to stop mid-blast. With all the physicians running to respond to the emergency, and all the kibbitzers and rubberneckers running along behind them, there was barely a minyan left.

Occasionally, accidents do happen, but fortunately medical assistance is never far off. Even if there were no members of the staff around, the Ace Bandage Brigade is always well represented. They are the "professional patients," the ones who've had — or witnessed — so many medical procedures that they know exactly what to do in an emergency. One time, an elderly gentleman leaned too far forward for *Modim* and, *nebach*, fell out of his wheelchair. Fortunately, he only sprained his wrist, and the patient next to him had a spare bandage in his *tallis zeckel*.

I T ALL MUST SOUND a bit chaotic, but if anything, it's a controlled chaos. The chief controller is Reb Michoel, an elderly, bewhiskered, Russian immigrant who, at his own initiative, runs the show — on a volunteer basis. With a congregation such as his, the ability to improvise is an obvious asset and there was never an improvisator more innovative.

The shul, with all its jury-rigged appurtenances, is tacit testimony to Reb Michoel's creativity, but his presence is felt even beyond these four walls. His influence extends to every area of religious observance within the hospital.

On Friday nights, he sleeps at Hadassah where he has his own room. Pounding his beat along each corridor in every ward, Michoel dispenses *lechem mishna* to all who wish, and to all he can cajole into the mitzva.

His specialty is *ex nihilo*: He produces carfare home for those who arrived with empty pockets on Shabbos and can even make those elusive telephone tokens materialize when you need them most. If a patient's escort or next-of-kin needs a bed for the night, Michoel can arrange it: In addition to having two spares in his room, he apparently has mastered the "shmear" technique of circumventing hospital regulations. His currency is his irresistible personality and obvious sincerity.

Michoel's Shabbos-hot-tea-with-no-*shailos*-and-plenty-of-sympathy-on-the-side has brought solace to countless infirm of body and spirit. He understands that melancholy often creates diseases which warmth and commiseration can cure.

An over-*Yom Tov* stay in the hospital is something anyone would want to avoid, if given the choice. Not Michoel. He's on the spot with a lulav, matza, Chanukah candles, or whatever it takes to help you remember the day and forget where you are.

O N ROSH HASHANAH Reb Michoel is the self-appointed First Lieutenant of the regiment of walking-wounded. The *shofar* is his bugle with which to herald their assembly. But the military imagery dissolves at the first *Mi Shebairach*. For Michoel, the prayer for a speedy recovery is not a duty to be fulfilled, or even an honor awarded, but a heartfelt supplication and sincere expression of compassion. He'll never become inured to the suffering of his congregants. Accustomed as they are to the perfunctory *Mi Shebairach* chant, none would deny that the honest emotion with which Michoel invests his prolonged recital is no less than a true reflection of their own fervent prayers:

"He who blessed our fathers, Avraham, Yitzhak, and Yaakov, Moshe and·Aharon, Dovid and Shlomo, may He heal..."

In times of unusual military tension, Reb Michoel invokes with great passion the Lord's blessings on "the soldiers of Israel guarding our borders from Lebanon to the Egyptian desert, from the Great Sea to the Arava..." When the occasion calls for it, he might even compose his own more original version of the prayer:

"...May the Holy One, blessed be He, have mercy and hastily restore ___ to perfect health, both spiritual and *physical; awaken him to* teshuva, *restore him to a Torah path, enable him to provide* nachas *and joy to his family and the Jewish people, banish our enemies... Amen."*

Despite his creative genius Reb Michoel does not have a monopoly on instilling *kavana*. The surroundings alone are adequately inspiring and suffuse the prayers with deep meaning.

"On Rosh Hashanah it is inscribed... who will live and who will..." "Our Father, Our King, send a speedy recovery to the ailing..." "God, forgive us please but not through suffering and affliction!" "Inscribe us in the Book of Life..."

A PARABLE is told to explain King David's perplexing verse in Psalms: *va'ani tefilla* — "and I am prayer." It may also explain the aura of *kavana* which fills the "other" Hadassah Synagogue.

A starving beggar lived on the outskirts of town. His robe was in tatters, his stomach bloated and hair matted. He was filthy and unkempt. He spent his days rummaging through garbage in search of scraps of food.

One day, the king came to town. In honor of this momentous occasion, he promised to grant a request to anyone who would appear before him and simply state his desire. The beggar was encouraged to make the journey and ask for the king's assistance. Barefoot and wearing his only rag of clothing across his emaciated torso, the poor man made the long, wearying climb to the house where the king lodged. He didn't even have in mind what he would ask of the king, only that the monarch relieve his misery.

At last he arrived, trembling from the exertion as much as from fear. "Your Majesty," he began.

"Say no more," the king interrupted in a gentle tone. "You need not tell me what it is you require, for it is most apparent."

So said King David: "O Lord, look upon me! My very *being* is the essence of prayer."

And that's the way it is at the "other" Hadassah Synagogue. These worshipers needn't say: "I stand before You *k'cheres hanishbar,* like a shattered vessel." The Almighty can see that; what they require is "most apparent." Even if they were unable to vocalize the words inscribed in the prayer books, their plastic tubes and sutures and pacemakers would be sufficiently eloquent, and a poignant reminder of man's vulnerability.

on Deliverance

שובי נפשי למנוחיכי כי ד' גמל
עליכי. כי חלצת נפשי ממות את
עיני מן דמעה את רגלי מדחי

תהילים קטז : ז

*Return to your rest, my soul;
for the Lord has provided
bountifully, you have delivered
my soul from death, my eyes from
tears, and my feet from falling.*

Psalms 116:7

Escape from bondage and servitude, from depravity and iniquity, from physical and spiritual oppression has characterized Jewish existence from biblical times to the present. We have ceased to wonder why the Chosen People were chosen for this particular role as well. Our souls only yearn for freedom — freedom to serve God in our own way.

Shackles and fetters and daunting circumstances can imprison the body but cannot restrain a spirit that strives for liberty. The amazing escapes from persecution our fellow Jews have executed in every part of the world are proof that no price is too dear to attain this precious goal.

KURDISTAN

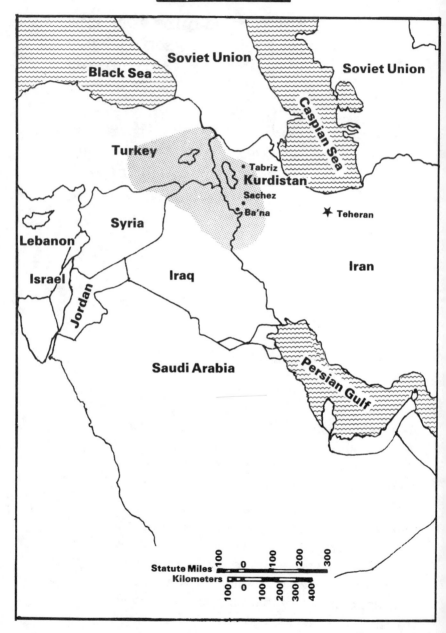

Where The Gold Is

(Bereishis 2:11)

BA'NA, Kurdistan in 1951 looked much as it had in 1851, or perhaps in 1051: homes were mud huts topped with dried straw domes; roads were dirt paths; plumbing, electricity, radios and cars were unheard of. Separated from its closest major city, Sachez, by a two-day donkey ride, Ba'na was a remote village near the Iran/Iraq border. Its isolation from twentieth century civilization, however, was absolute.

Many biblical scholars and archaeologists postulate that this fertile, verdant area where the Tigris and Euphrates flow is the site of the Scriptural Garden of Eden. The Jews of Ba'na were convinced of this long before the academicians.

Like the rivers of Paradise, the gentle stream that ambled through their town would regularly overflow its banks, irrigating fields and lush gardens. The receding waters deposited plump, rainbow-colored fish at their doorsteps and the villagers had only to step outside to collect their fresh dinner which lay flapping in the mud. The fragrance of apple blossoms, lilies and roses filled the air for miles around and the Jewish minority lived in apparent peaceful coexistence with their Moslem neighbors under the benevolent protection of the Shah.

The peace, however, was an uneasy one. Moslem and Jewish children played together often and visited in one another's home. The menfolk worked side by side in the open market stalls, sharing an easygoing camaraderie, while the women chattered and gossiped across adjoining backyards as they hung their wash to dry. Nonetheless the suppressed enmity was still palpable.

Despite the common language and lifestyle, the Jews retained their own distinct mode of dress, customs, and religious observance. Even their closest Moslem "friends" were not above tempting a young child with a piece of *treifa* meat — just for amusement, to be sure. And every Kurdistani Jew knew that his Moslem "friend" would not hesitate to turn against him, if such an act were in the Moslem's self-interest.

DURING THE YEARS of plenty, Moslem and Jew maintained the so-called peace. But there were years of drought and famine. At these times, the wild Kurdish tribes made forays from their mountain encampments into Ba'na to pillage and massacre the defenseless Jews. The victims' "friends" made themselves scarce, barricaded behind cellar doors, although there was little actual threat to their lives. Only on rare occasions could a Moslem body be found torn and bleeding in a ditch alongside that of his Jewish neighbor.

The members of the Jewish community were frequently compelled to flee for their lives to outlying settlements where they lived until the danger passed, sustaining themselves with the wild nuts and raisins that littered the ground. But when they returned to Ba'na, they found their fields burned and their homes looted. Their "friends" helped them rebuild and clucked sympathetically at their misfortune.

The drought that began in 1951 stretched on for year after year and the attacks became more frequent and brutal. There was not one Jewish family in all of Ba'na that hadn't lost a member to the rampaging Kurds. The Jews realized that they were soon to be expelled from "Paradise," but where would they go? Few had ever travelled beyond the outskirts of their village — perhaps greater terrors awaited them elsewhere?

They needed a place of refuge and tranquility, where there was no drought, famine or Kurds — and so they focussed their dreams on *Eretz Yisrael.* Not the nascent, independent State of Israel — they had no knowledge of current events or news of the world outside their boundaries — but the *Eretz Yisrael* of their fervent prayers, the land that flowed with milk and honey, the land God had bestowed upon His chosen people.

WHEN THE FIRST representative of the Jewish Agency, stationed in Teheran, arrived in the village in the early 1950s, he was greeted with incredulity. The very idea that their dreamland actually existed, that there were other Jews in the world besides themselves, that it was actually possible to go to this glorious place, hurled them into ecstasy. They spoke of nothing else. Who would go? When? How many? But these were unanswerable questions for impoverished peasants. The years of famine had taken their toll, chiseling away at their modest livelihoods.

Before morning prayers, the elders would discuss the prospects of *aliya*, but after weeks of debate it was clear that few if any of Ba'na's Jews could afford to emigrate. The rest would have to be patient and wait for better times. For the time being, they hung photographs of David Ben-Gurion, Chaim Weitzmann and Moshe Sharett in places of honor in the synagogue and kissed them whenever they passed by. And they continued to dream...

THE RABANNI FAMILY were among the dreamers, but for them it was truly no more than a dream. There were fourteen children (originally seventeen, but two infants and a ten-year-old had been murdered by the Kurds) and hardly enough food to go around. Many were the nights that Alya (Laya) and Eliyahu lay on their straw pallets with their stomachs rumbling from hunger. Alya was desolated to see her children grow thin and listless, barely more than skin and bones.

To add to her anguish, Alya had an ailing sister, Azib (Ziva), a widow with ten children of her own. Azib suffered from a debilitating disease and everyone knew she hadn't long to live. Whenever the Rabannis had any food to spare, Alya would carry pots of steaming rice to Azib's house to feed her starving brood.

As she lay dying, Azib beckoned her sister to her bedside and beseeched in a voice almost inaudible:

"Please, my dear Alya, promise me you will care for my children when I am gone."

Alya was appalled at the enormous burden this request placed upon her, for there was no alternative but to comply with her sister's wishes. What would Eliyahu say? Alya began to tremble with fear that he might turn her out if she were to bring home ten more mouths to feed. This was surely a death sentence for them all; there was no way the Rabannis could support twenty-four children!

Yet Alya could not refuse. She nodded once, and Azib sighed deeply, but before her soul departed, she opened her eyes once more.

"Alya, do not leave them behind when you go up to the Holy Land!"

Again Alya nodded, this time without hesitation: Azib could rest assured that her children would not be left behind. The addition of ten extra members to their already sizeable family virtually dashed whatever hopes the Rabannis had of ever leaving Ba'na.

ALYA HAD LITTLE time to grieve. She was overwhelmed with gratitude towards her husband who, like herself, could not deny Azib's children a home, and the very first priority was to arrange for her ten nieces and nephews to move in.

The Rabanni abode, a large thatch-roofed brick and mud two-story structure was a monument to their status during the years of plenty. In their current diminished circumstances, with many of their possessions already sold for food, if not stolen by the Kurds, finding space for the new arrivals and their pathetic collection of belongings was simple. The real problem was providing food and clothing.

ELIYAHU RABANNI was a "manna" merchant. Business was seasonal but profitable enough to support his family modestly all year on the income from one good harvest. In early spring, just after dawn, the fields surrounding the village became inundated with a thick layer of this blue-white crystalline substance, in places heaped as high as a small hillock. The family would gather great quantities of it for Eliyahu to sell in the *shuk*'s (open-air markets) of Sachez and Tabriz.

Scarce in the more populous locales, "arura" — manna — was highly valued for its unique flavor and consistency and was a favorite spread for pitta. None could say whether *arura* dropped off the trees, welled up from the earth, or fell from the sky, but whatever they did not gather and store, melted by midday and disappeared without a trace. For obvious reasons, the Jews of Ba'na called this delicacy "*mahn.*"

But even a bumper crop would not suffice to support the Rabannis' burgeoning household. Eliyahu set his businessman's mind to work on the problem.

Through his *shuk* connections, he arranged for his older nephews and sons to be apprenticed to other Jewish merchants and artisans: Yiftach at the silversmith, hammering leaves of precious metal to be shaped into ornate jewelry and *tashmishei kedusha*; Rachamim at the tobacconist sweeping sawdust from the carving of long, intricately designed pipes; Chofni at the textile dealer and his twin brother, Pinchas, at the *"Chacham,"* learning to be a scribe, and so on. Although they would earn no wages, their masters were obliged to provide meals.

The nieces, of course, did not leave the vicinity of the house but joined the Rabanni daughters in the traditional domestic arts of cooking and baking, cleaning, weaving and embroidering. Azib's thirteen-year-old daughter had a particular talent for embroidery and Eliyahu discovered that he could get a fair price for the lovely peacock-and-flower designs she created. This small bonus, along with the *mahn* income and the apprenticeships, enabled the Rabannis to survive.

BUT ONE OF Azib's boys, the one called Koma for his extraordinarily dark skin ("koma" means black), could not be apprenticed. He was a big, strapping lad of fifteen with good muscles in his arms and chest and broad, straight shoulders, but his mind was that of a five-year-old. He was wild and undisciplined and was constantly causing trouble, yet Alya had a soft place in her heart for him. Sometimes Koma would sit quietly beneath the *Chabusha* tree and play his *jirne* flute, but a moment later he might run screaming through the house, leaving a broken loom and overturned bowls of rice in his wake.

To keep him out of mischief, Alya set him to work turning the earth for the planting of a vegetable garden. True, it was unlikely that anything would ever grow there now that the river was no more than a trickle and the rainy season long past, but it kept him busy. Under her watchful eye, Koma worked like a demon, ploughing great furrows in the arid Kurdistani soil. His great pride in this simple triumph made her love him even more. She knew she had done the right thing by giving him a proper home — no matter the cost. What would have become of him, she dared not think.

O NE MORNING, Alya heard Koma shouting from the garden and she hurried from the kitchen to see what had disturbed the boy. Were the Kurds after him? Her heart raced.

To her astonishment, she found Koma leaping and dancing about the yard crying "*Lirei, lirei!*" She quickly tried to silence him for it was dangerous to attract this sort of attention from their Moslem neighbors, but Koma was uncontrollable. For the benefit of passersby, she pantomimed that the boy was demented while pushing him inside and latching the door.

"What's that you're hiding in your pocket?" she cajoled gently. Koma relinquished his precious find: a small gold coin! Alya flew from the house to the yard and searched for the spot where Koma had been digging, and there she discovered a treasure that boggled the mind: an old clay jug filled to overflowing with gleaming gold coins!

That night, by the light of the moon, four Rabanni children stood guard while their ten siblings and ten cousins in absolute silence dug up the entire yard. They dug with their bare hands so as not to make a sound; the hours passed quickly and the children worked feverishly. Eliyahu nervously smoked his *chargilla* and read the *kameah* blessing that hung on the wall.

With torn nails and bleeding fingers the children brought their finds to Alya, who sat on the doorstep with a dark dress spread out in her lap to hold the rapidly growing hoard. By dawn, the spark of the Rabannis' dream of settling in the Holy Land, long dimmed by poverty and travail, was rekindled: Koma's clay jug was the first of six identical vessels, all crammed with gold "lirei."

THIS, then, was Alya's and Eliyahu's reward for the years of sacrifice, for the care and love they showered upon their nieces and nephews. This was Koma's repayment for the special attention and affection he had never before received — Koma had given them back their dream. No one questioned the miraculous appearance of the treasure — is it not written: "A river issues forth from Eden to water the Garden... where the gold is" (*Bereishis* 2:11)?

Eliyahu and his eldest son Rafael, achieved their own minor miracle in an amazingly short time. With plenty of "baksheesh" to expedite the bureaucratic procedures, only two months passed before the appropriate officials were duly bribed and passports and documents acquired.

They told no one of their plans. Day after day, the girls stitched gold coins into pillows and linings while Eliyahu and Rafael made arrangements for a camel caravan to carry the Rabannis and their belongings to Sachez. Night after night the boys built crates from scrap wood and cord, and Alya carefully packed these with only the barest essentials. So many cherished heirlooms would have to be left behind, but how much could six camels carry?

O N MAY 30th, 1953, Alya, Eliyahu, twenty-four children aged five to seventeen, thirty-five exquisite rugs, numerous bolts of handwoven fabric, a few crates of copper cooking utensils, embroidered cushions, *kameahs*, elaborately illuminated handwritten *sefarim*, one colorful *ketuba** and several silk *tallitot* began their long and arduous journey.

Ahmed demanded an outrageous price for his silence and cooperation, but Eliyahu had been assured that he was a man of honor. He appeared just after dark with his camel herd and the Rabannis worked swiftly to load their belongings, food and the small children onto the animals lumpy backs.

Alya instructed Koma to feed and water the beasts, an activity that would keep them all — Koma included — quiet. At last, without even a backward glance, the Rabannis set off on their nocturnal trek.

They travelled only by night and rested by day in caves or under hastily pitched tents. The family reached Sachez in only three days, arriving just in time to catch the bi-weekly bus to the capital.

---

* The Jews of Kurdistan speak the *Sefaradit* dialect of Hebrew. Some transliterations in this story, therefore, appear in the *Sefaradit* form.

They tipped Ahmed handsomely and boarded their very first motorized vehicle — an experience that would have been petrifying had they not been so exhausted. As it was, they all slept for the duration of the eight-hour ride to Teheran.

Pinchas, who had studied with the *Chacham*, was the only Rabanni who could read and write. He had been charged with the responsibility of corresponding with the Jewish Agency office, but no one could be sure that the message had been received — until the men with the open-collared white shirts and the peculiar accents greeted the Rabannis as they piled off the bus.

T EHERAN was a dazzling, bewildering metropolis, but they had no opportunity to absorb the strange sights and sounds. They were shepherded into the belly of a giant silver eagle, their eyes riveted to the sky-blue *magen dovid* on its tail — a symbol so familiar and beloved that it calmed their fears.

With a prayer of thanksgiving on their lips, the Rabannis bid a final farewell to their Kurdistani Paradise, the land where the Tigris and Euphrates flow, the land where the gold was...

EPILOGUE: Twenty-three of the children eventually married and Alya disbursed the remains of the treasure among them. They all put their hard-earned skills to good use in the Holy Land: Yiftach became a renowned silversmith; three sons run a successful oriental carpet firm; Miriam and Tzophnat have a boutique in Haifa famous for its delicately woven and embroidered kaftans; two other children are partners in a popular Tel Aviv Kurdish restaurant; Pinchas is a *sofer*; another son is a rabbi; several learn in a Jerusalem *kollel*; and Rafael, who apparently inherited his father's business acumen and his mother's penchant for *gemilut chassadim*, owns a bookbindery where Koma and a dozen other mentally and physically handicapped young adults are gainfully employed.

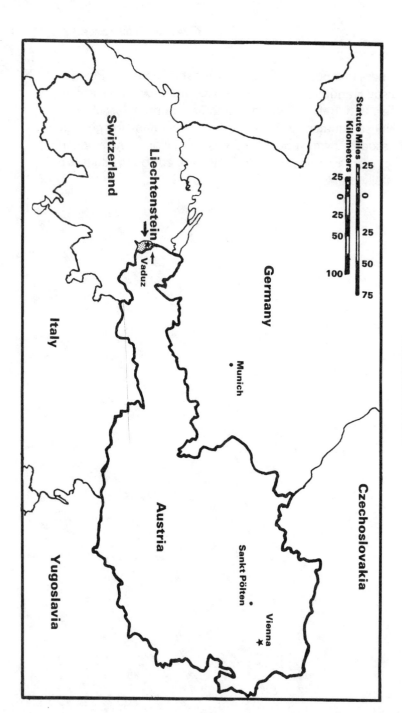

The Kartoffel Caper

"Watch out, *Herr Baron!*" cried the concierge. A runaway truck was hurtling down Kaernstrasse at break-neck speed. The concierge flew from his post to snatch the wealthy patron from the truck's path, where he had fallen.

Rottmann, still dazed, lifted himself up painfully from the street and then stooped to help his rescuer. "Franz, are you all right?"

"*Ya, ya mein Herr,*" replied the concierge, dusting off Rottmann's fur coat. "And you?"

"Thanks to you, Franz, I am uninjured. But tell me, what made you risk your life to save me?"

The two men limped slowly back to the hotel entrance. "Of all the visitors in this hotel, you, *mein Herr Baron*, are the only one who knows my name. To everyone else I am 'invisible,' a part of the stonework."

And thus was sown the seed of Rottmann's getaway plan.

The next day, Rottmann stopped to buy a newspaper at the stand on the corner. "*Guten Morgen*, Kurt," he greeted the old paper-seller. The wizened septuagenarian tipped his greasy cap and grinned. "I hope you make another fortune today, *Herr Baron*." The man's effusiveness made Rottmann stop and think. "And how is your little grandson's broken leg, Kurt?"

"The boy is fine, *danke shön. Herr* Rottmann, you are a very special man. I don't believe even one other of my regular customers would remember my face, let alone remember my troubles."

And thus the seed of Rottmann's getaway plan germinated.

I t was February 1937, and the stench of anti-Semitism filled the air in Vienna. The ineffectual Austrian chancellor Schuschnigg was fighting a losing battle against the Nazi scourge and *Sturmabteiling* stormtroopers terrorized Austria's streets with impunity. The day Rottmann had seen the little Jewish bookshop owner down on his hands and knees scrubbing the sidewalk — at gunpoint! — he'd known the end was not far off.

He had immediately sent his wife and children on a "ski vacation" to St. Moritz, dismissed the servants, and moved into the Sacher Hotel in the First District. There, he hoped, among the truly affluent of Vienna, he would be less conspicuous, and therefore less vulnerable, than in his own home. Aware that this was no more than a stopgap measure, he'd racked his brain for a fool-proof escape scheme.

Franz the doorman and Kurt the newspaper seller had unknowingly supplied the first tiny fertile spore. Now he wired his wife instructions to take a long-term lease on a *chalet*, and quietly began to liquidate his assets.

The sudden appearance of large blocks of stock on the international markets would have aroused suspicion. Similarly, word of Rottmann's properties and other holdings changing hands would draw undesirable attention to himself and the authorities might decide to scrutinize more minutely the genealogy of the noted entrepreneur and philanthropist. He could not be sure how much longer he could successfully conceal his background and remain at liberty and unharassed. The arrest of his colleague Zimmermann only a week before was a blood-chilling warning which Rottmann fully intended to heed.

Only twenty-four hours earlier he'd *davened Maariv* with Zimmermann and they'd dined together at the Hammerpurgstallgasse. Now both the Schiff Shul and the kosher restaurant were off-limits for Rottmann. In fact, he decided to keep his distance from Schiffstrasse altogether. Fortunately, produce that was scarce all over Austria was available in abundance at the Sacher and the *maître d'* was most accommodating to his "vegetarian" guest.

THE PROCESS of thawing frozen assets secretly was a long and tedious one. Each sale had to be executed through trusted intermediaries, but these days, who could be trusted? He riffled through folder after folder of stocks, bonds, title deeds and bank records, calculating the maximum he could hope to accumulate in the shortest space of time. He still had no idea how he would be able to transfer large sums abroad, but he would cross that bridge when he came to it.

There was no longer any question about whether he would try to escape — only the details had to be worked out. Because his face was so well-known, he could not possibly risk simply hopping aboard a train. And then there was the matter of the money: he would need several pieces of luggage to carry it and that would surely raise eyebrows...

By April, Rottmann had amassed over five hundred thousand dollars-worth in negotiable currency and he began to purchase fine diamonds and rare stamps — the most readily transportable legal tender in the world. Although he realized he could not chance carrying them on his person, lest he be searched, it gave him a good feeling to know he was one step closer to leaving. Then tragedy struck.

A TELEGRAM arrived from Munich advising him of his father's demise. In carefully shrouded language, the cable warned him that it was unsafe to attempt travelling to Munich for the funeral. Rottmann called his business office and delegated authority to his managing director while he stayed at home for a week "with a cold."

Rottmann sat *shiva* in his hotel room with only his loyal valet, Josef, for company. He received no callers and had all his meals delivered by Room Service. On the fourth day, Josef looked at his employer with surprise and said, "Please, *mein Herr*, if I did not know it was you, I would not have recognized your face!"

Running a hand over the growth of beard that covered his usually clean-shaven face, Rottmann could only imagine what Josef was talking about. It wasn't until after the *shiva* that he saw for himself.

The image reflected in the bathroom mirror was not *Herr Baron* Rottman, the wealthy tycoon, but a disheveled, middle-aged fellow with a scraggly grey-streaked beard.

Thus the seed of Rottmann's getaway plan took root.

On the first Sunday in May, Rottmann asked Josef to drive him into the country. The air smelled fresh as newly-cut grass as they drove casually along the road parallel to the railroad tracks. When they approached a sharp bend in the road just outside of Sankt Pölten, Rottmann saw a shabbily dressed tramp leap out from among the bushes and grab a handhold on the passing Arlberg Trans-Austrian Express, which had slowed for the turn.

Thus the seed of Rottmann's getaway plan sent forth a tender shoot.

I T WAS a humid morning in July when Rottmann witnessed the seizure of a guest in front of the hotel. The S.A. stormtroopers appeared suddenly, grabbed the man by the arms and bundled him into a waiting car. Rottmann was so shaken that he spun around, pulled his hat brim lower over his face, and hurried up the street. Inadvertently, he bumped into a greengrocer's potato stand.

"*Meine Kartoffeln!*" shouted the grocer. "*Dummkopf...* Oh, *Herr Baron!* Pardon me, please! I did not notice it was you..."

Rottmann realized how foolish he must have looked, scuttling up the street like a sneak-thief. He subdued his nervousness and calmly replied: "No, no, *Verzeihung*, it is I who must beg your pardon. I was not looking where I was going. I will of course reimburse you for the potatoes I knocked down."

But the grocer wouldn't hear of it. In fact, he quickly threw a number of "*Kartoffeln*" into a paper sack and pressed Rottmann to accept them. Not wishing to add insult to injury, Rottmann took the bag, slipped a fifty-schilling note onto the stand, and returned to the Sacher to rid himself of his burden. As he was about to discard them in the trash bin, a sudden thought occurred to him.

Using a fruit knife from the bowl on the sideboard, he gingerly sliced open one of the potatoes, hollowed out the center, and carefully fitted the two halves back together. "*Wunderbar!*" he exclaimed, smiling in triumph.

And thus the seed of Rottmann's getaway plan blossomed in all its glory.

I N LATE AUTUMN, Rottmann counted up his holdings. He had converted over two million dollars into diamonds and stamps. And in the bottom of a locked wardrobe in his bedroom was an even more precious hoard: several dozen earth-impacted potatoes of various vintage.

Every night before he went to sleep he carved a small hollow in the center of another of his potatoes and filled it with a two- or three-carat stone or a well-wrapped stamp, and then fitted the halves precisely together. By smearing the soil with his finger, he was able to camouflage the seam. There were more potatoes than he could possibly require, but Rottmann believed they might come in handy all the same.

Since his first Sunday country visit back in May, Rottmann had turned it into a ritual: each week he had Josef take him for a leisurely drive to Sankt Pölten. He had purchased a large wooden case filled with painting equipment and would ask Josef to let him off at some scenic spot where he could pursue his new "hobby." For a few minutes he'd daub pigment on a canvas, and then quietly sit refining and savoring his cleverly conceived scheme.

THE LATE WINTER rainstorms interrupted Rottmann's "painting" routine but gave him an idea for the final, elusive element in his elaborate escape plan. He sent word on Friday to Kurt the newspaper seller asking that he deliver the morning paper to Rottmann at the hotel. When the old man tapped tentatively on the door, Rottmann invited him in for breakfast.

"Kurt, my good man, you have done me a great service. Now I would like to return the favor." Kurt began to protest but Rottmann was insistent. "It pains me to see you standing on the cold street corner each day in nothing but rags. Please accept this new suit of warm clothing and this heavy overcoat."

The paper-seller was speechless. Too frightened to refuse, he began to shuck his tattered clothes and don Rottmann's magnanimous gift. *"Mein Herr Baron,* this is too — too fine for me," he stammered. But Rottmann prevailed and saw the old fellow to the door. Then he added Kurt's rags to his private cache.

Rottmann's blossoming getaway plan was ready to be plucked — and none too soon.

Later that morning, he called his office once again with orders for his managing director to take over for a few days.

"*Herr Baron*," the director whispered conspiratorially, "some men were here asking questions..." Then the line went dead. Rottmann replaced the receiver with a trembling hand.

A moment later, when he had regained his composure, he turned to Josef and said ever-so-casually, "Do you know, I rather liked the way I looked in that beard. I think I shall grow one again." The expression in Josef's pale blue eyes was all Rottmann needed to tell him who had betrayed him. He kept a close watch on his "loyal" valet all weekend, not letting Josef out of his sight for a minute.

When he left the Sacher that Sunday — a year to the day since he'd first checked in — he wore his coat collar high over his chin and a wide silk scarf wrapped across his cheeks. Josef had brought the car around and stowed the artist's case in the back seat as Rottmann had requested. As they pulled away from the curb, a dark sedan drew up... Rottmann told his driver to accelerate.

As soon as they arrived at Rottmann's "favorite" spot along the country lane, he got out and, carrying the case — now containing Kurt's rags and an old sack filled with his treasured tubers — strolled nonchalantly through the meadow.

THE CONDUCTOR marched through the cars of the long train, perusing documents and punching tickets. "*Nein, Fräulein*," he told a young woman, "the border crossing at Liechtenstein will take no time at all. It is only a formality there." He glanced at his large gold pocketwatch. "We should be in Vaduz in less than two hours."

"*Ach du Lieber!* An honest citizen must pay his whole

salary for a ticket these days," an elderly passenger complained to the conductor, "while tramps ride the rails for free."

"No bums ride *my* train for free!" the conductor proclaimed emphatically, and began to search for one just in case.

Two S.A. stormtroopers were checking identity papers when the conductor approached. "Perhaps you have seen a freeloader in the course of your examinations?" he asked. The soldiers laughed. "We are looking for a much bigger fish: Rottmann — that money-grubbing *Schweinhund.*"

"And you think he is on *my* train?" The conductor puffed out his chest self-importantly. "We will search together! It shouldn't be too difficult to spot that face — or just look for a fur coat with hundred-schilling notes sticking out of the bulging pockets." The soldiers patted the trainman on the back and chuckled.

THEY INSPECTED every passenger coach and then began on the freight cars, probing under bundles and behind crates. In the last car, in the darkest corner, they found him.

In that moment Rottmann knew that his life depended on an extra measure of Divine assistance — and that he would have to earn. He mentally pledged vast sums to *tzedaka* in the hope that this would qualify him for the special protection awarded to mitzva emissaries. And *if* he reached his destination safely, he would spare no effort to save his widowed mother, he vowed, remembering the scriptural reward: "so that your days may be long..."

"So, we've caught your tramp," the troopers said to the conductor. "What do you have to say for yourself, you old wretch?"

"*Bitte, Oberleutnant*, please sir, I am but a poor farmer. What do you want of me?"

"A poor farmer, eh? You think that gives you the right to ride the railroad without paying? What are you, a thieving Jew?"

Rottmann spat on the floor in apparent disgust, but said nothing. One of the soldiers kicked him with his heavy boot. "If you're not a thieving Jew, you must be a Jewish pig — dirtying a nice clean train that way. Mop that up at once!" Rottmann wiped his spittle with his sleeve.

"**M**AYBE THIS IS *'Herr Baron'* Rottmann!" the lieutenant jeered. "Just look at his finely-tailored suit, *nicht wahr?*" The three manhunters guffawed loudly. Rottmann stopped breathing.

"And what do you have in that sack, you filthy beggar?" the second soldier demanded. "And you had better not lie, or we will *know* you are a Jew!" He swatted Rottmann's jaw with his gun butt, knocking out a tooth.

"Sir, it is *Kartoffeln*... just, just some potatoes."

"So, potatoes. Let's take a look, *ya?*" The soldier stabbed his bayonet into the sack, splitting the threadbare fabric. The blood froze in Rottmann's veins as a small spud rolled out. Perspiration burst from every pore, soaking his collar and dripping down his back. The train made a sharp turn and the potato slammed into the iron door... and split open.

"*Gott in Himmel!* What is that repulsive smell?" The soldiers and the conductor fled from the reeking car. "Leave that stinking bum and his rotten, stinking potatoes!"

Rottmann's heart was beating again. He rocked on his heels and laughed long and heartily... as the train rolled across the border into Liechtenstein — two weeks ahead of the *Anschluss*.

MOROCCO

France

Marseilles

Atlantic Ocean

Portugal

Spain

Mediterranean Sea

Tangiers

Rabat

Algiers

Casablanca

Oran

Morocco

Fez

El Aricha

Marrakech

Tizi n' Tichka Pass

High Atlas Mountains

Oued Ziz river

Béchar

Algeria

Sahara

Statute Miles 100   0   100   200   300
Kilometers 100   0   100   300

Flight From Fez

"*LA BES*, ABU-YOSEF," Eliezer hailed his cousin through the doorway of the tiny leather goods shop on Fatima Street.

Chaim Benita looked up from his work. "Welcome, my friend, come in and sit a while." Everyone in the Fez "mellah" called Chaim "Abu-Yosef" — the father of his first-born son, Yosef. "Will you have a cup of mint tea?"

"Abu-Yosef, how can you talk of mint tea? Haven't you heard? Those vicious murderers burnt down Suissa's store early this morning — with old Jacques still inside!"

"Yes, Eliezer, I heard. But King Hassan is sworn to protect us. I am certain his troops will soon restore order..."

"No, Cousin!" Eliezer leaped from his seat, overturning the stool with the force of his frustration. Abu-Yosef's equanimity was infuriating. "You must stop avoiding the truth: no one — not even the 'great' Hassan — can control these ruthless demons. The Illuz family is still in mourning for their daughter — she was only a *child*, Abu-Yosef! Hacked to pieces — in broad daylight!"

"Calm yourself, Eliezer. There is nothing we can do. The Almighty will not abandon us," Benita said with quiet assurance.

"The Almighty sends us a sign, Cousin. He is telling us it is time to leave this wretched place." He turned to go. "You are either too blind to see, or you are a fool," he added in disgust.

BENITA STAYED HIM with a hard look. "Eli, we are not just cousins, we have been friends for a lifetime. I know you do not think me a fool any more than I do you. It is neither foolishness nor blindness that keeps me from leaving — but fear." He hesitated, knowing that the news he was about to report would be devastating. "I overheard two Arab customers talking..." He placed a work-worn hand on Eliezer's broad shoulder. "The *Pisces*... pirates sank the ship, forced it onto the rocks. They said all the passengers who did not drown... were shot."

Eliezer stared at his friend in disbelief and then buried his face in his hands and cried with despair. "My nephew," he sobbed, "and his young wife! They were on that boat! No, no, it cannot be, it cannot be!"

"It is true, Cousin. It is one thing to be allowed to emigrate and quite another thing to be *able* to. We must wait." Then he lowered his voice and said: "I have been in touch with the men from the Jewish Agency. If anyone can get us out of here safely, I believe it is they."

"Abu-Yosef! Why did you not tell me before?"

"Keep your voice down, Cousin," Benita whispered urgently, "the Istiqlal have agents everywhere! I will tell you the moment I hear from my contact. Until then, you must not utter a word of this to anyone." The men embraced briefly and Eliezer stepped furtively out onto the street.

FROM THE TIME Morocco became a French Protectorate in 1912, Fez was its cultural capital, and by 1960 it was a thriving metropolis. The sophisticated architecture of museums, theaters and universities lined the city's ancient streets and sculptured fountains graced its squares. Opulent marble-tiled interior courtyards of palatial residences could be seen through elegantly carved entrance gates. And inside these homes, gleaming white walls set off furnishings and carpets of breathtaking beauty.

Not far from the heart of this gilt-edged municipality, but lightyears away in terms of affluence and prosperity, lay the "mellah," the Jewish ghetto of Fez — a blot on the glittering cityscape. The dazzling North African sun never reached the mellah, where precariously tall wood houses cast long shadows on dismal cobblestoned streets. Fifty thousand Fez Jews, a fractional minority among their five million Arab hosts, occupied an area of four square-blocks.

Despite the squalor of the mellah, for many years the community enjoyed a vibrant and active Jewish existence. Yeshivas, *chadorim,* ("kutabs") shuls and *mikvaos* were abundant and there was no dearth of learned scholars and rabbinic leaders. During the reign of Sultan Mohammed V, a somewhat enlightened despot, the Jewish third-class citizens of Morocco flourished.

For reasons known only to himself, and in contradiction to the tenets of Islam, the Sultan chose not to annihilate the "infidels," but to allow them a modicum of freedom — within the confines of the mellah. To the Jews of Morocco, isolation from their Moslem Arab neighbors was a welcome blessing: the less they had to do with them — the better.

BEFORE HIS DEMISE in 1961, Mohammed V extracted a solemn oath from his son to carry on his liberal policies toward the Jews, whom he viewed as a talisman. Hassan II reluctantly agreed, intending no more than passive compliance.

When he ascended the throne, in order to assuage Jewish fears that "a new king who knew not Joseph" had come to power, he lifted the Arab League-imposed ban on emigration to Israel. Unbeknownst to Hassan, this token concession — of which few impoverished Moroccan Jews could avail themselves — was the spark that ignited a conflagration: the Istiqlal reign of terror.

Istiqlal, the militantly radical opposition party, sought to undermine and eventually overthrow the monarchy — by any means — and the Jewish beneficiaries of Hassan's munificence became their primary targets. Istiqlal thugs — Moslem extremists who needed little incitement to arouse their hatred and lust for Jewish blood — were unleashed on the defenseless mellah. And life in the ghetto became a nightmare.

ABU-YOSEF BENITA was outwardly calm and self-assured, but his composure had no noticeable effect on the tension-charged atmosphere in the crowded room. He scanned the anxious faces of the twenty-three men seated in a wide circle of cushions all around him: his younger brothers and nephews, his cousins, his daughters' husbands, and finally his own twelve sons.

All those present respected him and looked to him for guidance. They would abide by his decision without question or debate. The onus of responsibility for the lives of these men, their women and children, weighed heavily on Benita's shoulders.

THE EVENTS of the past two weeks had etched deep furrows in his brow and cheeks. It was no longer a matter of isolated incidents of terror: the Istiqlal was wreaking havoc in the mellah and each unavenged act emboldened them to perform even greater atrocities.

The Istiqlal had proclaimed one morning that Jews were forbidden on the streets that day — under penalty of death. The edict was announced only after the younger children had left for school and the Benitas had been compelled to smuggle them home one by one under the voluminous dress of their Moroccan employee. Three neighbors' children were brutally slain in the gutter, and their hideously mutilated bodies could not be retrieved until nightfall.

The animals had then turned their voracious jaws on Amar, the jeweler. When he had stooped to remove an item from a lower shelf, they had pulled out an axe and chopped off his head! Now all that remained of Yehoshua Amar was an orphaned family, a barred and shuttered storefront, and a bloodstained sidewalk on Fatima Street.

The Istiqlal was a raging monster, growing in size with every Jewish body it devoured, and the community was powerless to defend itself. As so many times before in history, the Jews were caught in the crossfire: the frontline casualties in a violent political struggle.

If the Istiqlal succeeded in deposing the king, the Jews were doomed. Playing the role of cannon-fodder for their passive "protector" was no less a death sentence. Their only hope was escape.

WITH THE EYES of all his family upon him, Abu-Yosef drew a deep breath and announced: "We go." The women, eavesdropping from the kitchen doorway, began to ululate* with joy, but Benita silenced them with a fierce glare. There would be time for rejoicing later, with God's help — if they arrived safely at their destination.

* An onomatopoeic word, "ululate" describes the high-pitched, warbling trill sounded by Oriental women as an expression of deep emotion.

There was good reason to doubt the outcome of their venture: A group of 1,400 Jewish *émigrés* had been intercepted by the Istiqlal while trying to board ships at Tangiers. The 1,400 had disappeared without a trace. From Jewish communities all over Morocco came countless reports of arrests and imprisonment of many who tried to leave. The Istiqlal had become a self-appointed "secret police," answerable to no one.

TWO MORE terror-filled weeks elapsed before Benita received word from his Jewish Agency contact. The terse message appeared on a slip of paper stuffed into a bale of leather that was delivered to his shop: "Prepare. (signed) Zioni." Their clandestine activities precluded the use of real names and all those involved in Morocco's "underground railway" to *Eretz Yisrael* were known simply as the "Zionim" or "Shlichim" (agents).

Benita destroyed the note and sent his son Yehuda to relay the message to the other members of the Benita party. Then he began in earnest to comply with the Zioni's instruction: He worked swiftly to stitch sturdy leather shoes and warm jackets of every size, completing the task he had begun even before announcing his decision to the family.

The long, nervous wait would soon be over. Their plans had to be kept a guarded secret, for the slightest hint could jeopardize the lives of not only those who wished to emigrate — but those who remained behind as well. One innocent slip of the tongue could be fatal. It was best not to sit idle now and the leather work was both productive and blessedly distracting.

Only eight days had passed since the heinous murder of his son-in-law: Aharon's knife-slashed body had been found impaled on a meathook in the back of his butcher shop.

Now Miriam was a widow at the age of eighteen and her unborn child was already an orphan.

I T WAS TEN O'CLOCK on Friday morning, a bitter cold day in December, 1962, when the *Shlichim* knocked on the door of the Benita home. Asher ran to the *shuk* to get his father, while the *Shlichim* paced the parlor floor impatiently.

Father and son quickly filled two large jute sacks with handmade leather goods and heaved them onto their backs. Abu-Yosef took one final glance around the tiny, scrap-strewn shop he'd inherited from his grandfather, sighed deeply, and locked up for what he knew instinctively was the last time.

Before allowing his guests to speak, Abu-Yosef served them hot, sweet coffee and almond pastries, and the *Shlichim*, despite the urgency of their mission, accepted his gracious hospitality. They knew it would be a long time before Abu-Yosef could again host visitors in his own home.

"Within twenty-four hours, you will leave Fez," one of the *Shlichim* said quietly as he rose to depart.

B ENITA STRUGGLED to conceal his dismay, but his guests' grim-faced expressions told him there was no room for negotiation. The idea of travelling on the Sabbath was appalling — surely the Zionim understood that? But could the Benitas risk postponement? How many more lives might be lost as a result?

His moment of indecision passed and Abu-Yosef suddenly became aware that this must be God's Will. His incisive mind was already at work planning the details of the Benitas' departure.

As soon as the *Shlichim* left, Naftali was dispatched to make the rounds to all the families' homes and after *Maariv* services, they gathered again at Abu-Yosef's house — sixty-two souls in all. Packing their scant belongings was of course out of the question; the Sabbath likewise precluded taking along provisions. Before candle-lighting, each family had set the customary pot of *chamin (cholent)* on the fire as a stratagem for deluding any curious neighbors whose suspicions might otherwise have been aroused.

Abu-Yosef distributed the thick-soled shoes and sheepskin-lined leather vests he had labored so diligently to finish in time. Until midnight, the Benitas prayed together for a safe journey and recited *Tehillim*. Then they lay down to rest, but poised as they were on the brink of the unknown, with terror at their backs and mortal dangers ahead, none could find respite. Only the innocent babies slept.

A T THREE O'CLOCK in the morning, Abu-Yosef heard the distant muffled sputtering of an aging motor. He roused the family, instructed the men to don their prayer shawls under their coats, and warned the children to remain absolutely silent no matter what. By the time the soft rapping sound came, they were ready.

An old, nondescript bus with blacked-out windows waited outside the house and the Benitas quietly filed aboard. The driver's seat was sealed off so that even the dimmed dashboard lights didn't help to illuminate the vehicle, and the family sat in total darkness, alone with their fright. What awaited them beyond their familiar borders? What route would they take? How long would the journey last? The *Shlichim*, in whom they had absolute faith, volunteered no answers to their unspoken questions.

Just after dawn, oranges were distributed, but the Benitas would not partake until they had finished *Tefilla*. Like most Oriental* Jews, they knew the text by heart, so the absence of *siddurim* posed no problem. When they completed their whispered prayers, they made "*kiddush*" over the fruit and then tried to sleep.

THE BUS CAME to a halt at eleven o'clock Saturday morning. The sudden bright sunlight that poured through the open door was blinding after so many hours in the gloom and the travellers blinked and squinted like moles emerging from subterranean burrows. Those closest to the front could see that the bus was parked somewhere on the outskirts of a major city, within sight of the port.

"*Shabbat shalom* — welcome to Casablanca!" Two young *Shlichim* scrutinized the group that had been placed in their safekeeping, and addressed them in the French-Arabic patois that was the language of the mellah.

"It was our intention that you remain here in Casablanca overnight. You were to have been made comfortable in the big synagogue and then board a ship to Tangiers tomorrow morning. Of necessity, however, the plans have been changed..."

THE *SHLICHIM* explained that a four-day African Summit Conference was slated to convene in Casablanca. A vanguard of Egyptian intelligence officers were arranging security measures for President Gamal

---

* "Oriental," or Eastern, Jewry (עדות המזרח) is the term applied to Jews from Asian and North African countries (Iraq, Yemen, Syria, Iran, Morocco, etc.). North African Jews, whose forebears were exiled from Spain and southern France at the time of the Inquisition, speak the *sefaradit* ("Spanish") Hebrew dialect. Some transliterations in this story, therefore, appear in the *sefaradit* form (*e.g., Shabbat, kippot*).

Abdel Nasser, creating an atmosphere of vigilance and a convenient smoke-screen for Istiqlal terrorism. As a result, some 2,000 Jews had already been arrested on trumped-up charges.

A drive had been launched against Jews wearing blue and white clothing, attire which ostensibly indicated pro-Israel sentiments. Men with black *kippot* or other black garments were detained and beaten for "displaying signs of mourning" at Nasser's visit. Worshipers en route to *Shabbat* services had been taken into custody while police had raided Jewish homes, apprehending over a hundred and fifty persons, and twenty yeshiva students had been tortured and imprisoned.

Casablanca's mellah was virtually under siege. Many had tried to escape by boat but Istiqlal pirates were on the prowl, commandeering ships and seizing "contraband" — the Jewish passengers.

SO YOU SEE, my friends," the *Shaliach* concluded, "we cannot risk travelling through pirate-infested waters. Now we must wait for further instructions — an alternate route." He glanced at his watch. "They are sure to arrive at any mo..." He stopped abruptly as a cloud of dust appeared on the road.

Abu-Yosef could see that the *Shaliach*'s report had had an unnerving effect on the family, and they would need all the courage possible to face the trials ahead. He gathered them around him and reminded them it was time for *Mincha* — they would soon be on their way again and might not have another opportunity. Once more, his reassuring demeanor stilled their fears.

The cloud of dust became a motorcade of ten "tourist taxis." As they pulled over onto the pavement, the black-windowed bus that had carried them from Fez drove off, its anonymous driver waving farewell to the Benitas through the window.

BEFORE THE BENITAS were permitted to board the cabs, the *Shlichim* examined them for any distinctive signs of Jewishness and instructed the women to remove their *magen-dovid* necklaces and other similarly designed jewelry. The men were told to hide their *kippot* and to shave off their beards and sidelocks.

In that moment, the enormity of their situation overwhelmed them. Cut off from friends and neighbors they'd known their whole lives and from the place they'd called home for generation after generation, they were now compelled to actively desecrate the Sabbath and violate the sacred Torah. It was as if their old existence had come to an end, while the new one was yet a long way off. With tears streaming down their faces, the Benitas complied.

THEY PILED into the "tourist taxis" for the lengthy trip to Marrakech. They were triangulating Morocco — from Fez in the interior, to Casablanca on the coast, and now back to the interior — and they were further away from their destination than when they had begun. A new group of *Shlichim* greeted them at Marrakech, and while they ate and drank their first sustenance in many hours, a *Shaliach* briefed them on their itinerary.

The plan entailed trekking by foot across the High Atlas Mountains, groping through an uncharted jungle, and fording the Oued Ziz river that would bring them to the Algerian border. To the Benitas, the proposition was more intimidating than a voyage through pirate-infested seas, and — like the Children of Israel in the wilderness — they wanted nothing more than to return to the "security" of the mellah.

"Others have done it before," the *Shaliach* said of the proposed six-hundred kilometer migration, "and I will be with you the whole way."

THE BENITAS had come to look upon the *Shlichim* as their saviors and the fact that one would be accompanying them gave them the extra boost they needed. "In that case," said Abu-Yosef, "join us for our evening prayers. You will be part of the family." After *Maariv*, they recited *Havdalah* over one of the torches that would light their way through the Moroccan night.

The *Shaliach* would not reveal his name so the Benitas called him "Ezra"* — for the invaluable assistance he provided. Ezra had located reliable, competent guides to lead the family on their expedition, and procured accurate maps and adequate supplies.

They were to travel only by night, when the Istiqlal menace was greatly reduced, but they had to contend with equally deadly hazards... The guides warned that the mountains could be treacherous at this time of year, with severe blizzards and sudden ice storms. But there was a short cut: the Tizi n' Tichka Pass, and this was the route agreed upon. It involved a minor detour to the south, adding some twelve hours to the trip, but would halve the total travel time.

EVEN IN THE FOOTHILLS of the majestic, snow-capped Atlas mountains, the climate was drastically colder than in Casablanca and the family was never more grateful to Abu-Yosef for thoughtfully providing the warm vests and heavy shoes. The Benitas were city-dwellers,

---

* The Hebrew word עזרה (*ezrah*), meaning "help" or "aid," is a homonym for the Scriptural name עזרא (Ezra).

inexperienced and unequipped to travel long distances over unfamiliar terrain on foot. Each step left deep impressions in the fresh snow, quickly obliterated by violent gusts of wind.

Ezra rigged slings for carrying the small children so the family was able to maintain a fairly brisk pace. They rested only once — just long enough to rub feeling back into numbed limbs — but the Arab guides had no pity: This, they claimed, was the "easiest" part of the trip.

B Y MORNING, they had traversed the mountains and descended into dense jungle, where new horrors awaited them. Without warning, low-hanging branches turned into venomous cobras. Winter-starved tigers roared not far enough away and jackals howled and laughed in anticipation of the feast they would enjoy the moment a Benita took one false step. Swarms of insects attacked them mercilessly, stinging every exposed piece of flesh. Eliezer, seeing how the family suffered, begged the guides to stop a while, but they said: "If we rest here, the mosquitoes will eat us alive." They pressed on.

But God was with them on every leg of the arduous route. When they emerged at last from the dark green opaqueness of the jungle, scratched and bleeding but *alive,* the star-studded Sahara sky glittered welcomingly. They fell to the ground with sheer exhaustion and relief, and thanked the Almighty for His benevolence and guidance.

I T WAS ALMOST NOON when the weary party arose to a broiling desert sun which erased all memory of winter. The family trudged through the sandy wasteland and waves of heat shimmered off the dunes. They had long since lost any sense of direction; only the guides knew the way to the river and the Benitas followed like mindless sheep.

When they happened on an abandoned goatskin tent large enough to accommodate them all, they were certain it was just another mirage. But the blessed shelter it provided was no figment of their imagination. The Benitas, Ezra and the two Arab guides collapsed into a deep sleep.

THE PARTY was awakened by a sound like thunder. Abu-Yosef rose quickly and peered out the flap of the tent and then began to quake with fear at the spectacle that met his aching eyes: riders — dozens of them — on camelback, galloping toward the tent at an incredible speed. And as they drew nearer, the sight of them struck terror in his heart. They looked like fiendish apparitions in blue: blue turbans, blue robes, blue faces and hands — even their wild, windblown beards were blue.

"Ai!" screamed one of the guides, "it is the 'Blue Men' — we are finished!" He grabbed his pack and fled, with the second Arab at his heels. Two riders veered off and gave chase, easily overtaking the runners. And then, two rifle shots...

The riders — over thirty men and animals — reined in at Abu-Yosef's feet. Their leader dismounted and came forward, his leathery, weather-worn face devilish and grotesque. The Benitas huddled in the farthest corner of the tent, too paralyzed with fright to utter a sound, but Abu-Yosef stood his ground.

THE BLUE MAN stretched out his hand and smiled a ghastly, toothless smile. "*Marchaba*," he said in Arabic, and Abu-Yosef automatically responded, "*Marchabtain*," offering his own hand in return.

"Those two were thieves and murderers. Last season, they stole six mounts and killed my son. Justice is swift in the desert, praise Allah."

"I would wish to offer more than my hand in gratitude," Abu-Yosef apologized, attempting to sound as convincing as possible, "but our supplies are gone. May 'Allah' shower you with blessings for rescuing us from those evil men." These words apparently had the desired effect on the blue sheik, for his face split into yet another horrid grin. He signalled to his men and they all dismounted.

"We camp tonight at the Oued Ziz," said the sheik. "Your tribe may ride with us."

Abu-Yosef hastily consulted with Ezra and Eliezer. "Without the guides, finding our way to the river will be difficult," Ezra responded. "We *must* go with them."

But Eliezer had misgivings: "Who are these desert-demons? Their friendly manner could be deceptive — lies come easily to such lips, as we all know so well. Perhaps our fate will be no less gruesome than that of our guides!"

"What you say is true, Cousin, but we dare not risk angering them by refusing. I, too, am afraid, but we are in God's hands and only He determines our fate." Abu-Yosef nodded to the sheik and then helped his family climb onto the crouching camels.

S HARING the blue sheik's saddle, Abu-Yosef noticed that his own hands had taken on a bluish tinge. It reminded him that the same phenomenon occurred whenever he worked with certain colored leathers. Obviously the blue tribe must use an indigo dye for their turbans and robes — no doubt to ward off the evil eye — and the color rubs off on their skin. He laughed out loud at his earlier superstitious foolishness.

The Blue Men carried the travellers to an oasis at the Oued Ziz. There the Benitas refreshed themselves in the cool waters and dined on wild dates and almonds, but the sheik and his tribe remained apart. When the sun rose the following morning, the Blue Men were gone and the Benitas resumed their journey with new vigor.

EZRA SELECTED the three boldest-looking men — Abu-Yosef, Eliezer and Reuven Benita — and handed each of them a counterfeit Tunisian passport. These solitary documents, accompanied by an ample cushion of "baksheesh," were supposed to get sixty-two men, women and children across the Algerian border, on the other side of the river. Ezra carefully briefed them on the plan of action.

At the border, the three passport-bearers carried the day: their glib tongues and forceful personalities occupied the border patrol long enough to smuggle the rest of the family through unnoticed. Perhaps it was the hefty bribe that induced the officers' temporary blindness, but, no matter — the important thing was that another hurdle was behind them.

SPURRED ON by their achievement, and with water bottles and food supplies replenished, they set out by truck for Béchar. The wheezing, rust-scarred, broken-down heap was designed to transport half the weight that was now demanded of it but it was the only vehicle Ezra could buy cheaply. Its bald tires easily lost traction on the sand-swept road and on eight separate occasions, the Benitas had to alight to wrestle the van back onto the pavement.

Arriving at Béchar the same evening, they spent the night in the truck and planned out the route to Oran. Before sunrise they were back on the road, but at El Aricha, the van's decrepit engine turned over for the last time. The shifting desert dunes soon gave it a decent burial and the family found itself once again on foot in the Sahara.

As they were about to set forth from El Aricha, a donkey herdsman appeared and graciously offered to hire out his animals. The Benitas — now experienced riders since their jaunt on camelback with the Blue Men — eagerly clambered aboard the hardy beasts. By midnight, they arrived in Oran and slept fitfully on the synagogue floor.

Ezra, however, had no time to sleep. He had to make contact with the *Shlichim* in Oran or his "family" would be stranded in Algeria, no better off than in Morocco. He sped to the rendezvous point — a small apartment over a bookshop in the center of town.

The proprietor of the bookshop who lived there was a well-paid informer. He greeted Ezra with shocking news: two *Shlichim* had been arrested and convicted of sedition, and were hanged that very morning. Ezra suspected the bookseller of double-dealing. Like any informer, he would provide information to whomever paid the higher price, and the *Shlichim* had apparently been outbid.

There was nothing he could do in Oran without his contacts and so he made his way back to the synagogue to apprise the Benitas. Early the next morning he hired cars to shuttle them to the port of Algiers, where other *Shlichim* were headquartered. Ezra's supply of bribe-money was running dangerously low; he prayed the desperate cable he'd sent to friends in the capital would bring results.

THE ROADS were good, for once, and reasonably free of traffic, and the Benitas reached the docks in less than three hours. They were nervous and overtired, spent after the harrowing mountain-jungle-desert experience, yet were unable to relax in the crowded, noisy cars.

At the bustling port of Algiers, the family was herded into a departure terminal to await examination by the emigration official. When the official arrived, resplendent in gold braid and starched white uniform, he took one look at their haggard faces and ragged passports and declared: "These documents are forgeries." He signalled for the harbor police.

Their strength depleted and their confidence shattered, the Benitas began to cry. After all they had endured they would now be thrown into an Algerian jail, to rot for God-only-knew how long. Or worse — tortured and hanged for treason like Ezra's comrades.

Abu-Yosef suppressed their self-pitying moans. "Did the Almighty not save us from the Istiqlal? Did He fail us in the snows of the mountains or the heat of the desert? Did He allow us to be devoured by wild beasts in the jungle? He will not abandon us now."

EZRA CARRIED ON a whispered conference with the emigration official and money changed hands. But it was not enough. He slipped off his watch and handed it to the civil servant, who inspected it... and returned it, shaking his head impatiently. Eliezer tried to help, adding his wife's thin gold necklace to the kitty, but the man was not impressed. All the while, the family offered up silent, urgent prayers.

Just then, a higher-ranking official entered the terminal, along with two well-dressed young men. Ezra's eyes lit up, but he said nothing. The negotiations proceeded in a rapid, unfamiliar dialect and fifteen minutes later, the Benitas were ushered through the main gate. But Ezra remained.

Abu-Yosef looked inquiringly at the young man whom he had come to think of as an adopted son. "I had hoped to travel with you," the *Shaliach* said with a catch in his voice, "but I must stay behind. There is still much work to be done..." The Benitas embraced him and cried at the loss of so great a friend. Embarrassed at his own display of emotion, Ezra hurried them onto the waiting merchant ship and waved from the pier. "May God be with you! *Shalom!*" The Benitas called back, "*Tizkeh l'mitzvot* — farewell until we meet again in *Eretz Yisrael!*"

THE VESSEL was hardly more than a leaking scow, and the family was stowed in the hold along with the rest of the cargo. The huge, massive-muscled black African sailors who manned the ship would not allow them up on deck, so they were forced to remain below in the stifling bowels of the boat. Despite their greater numbers, the Benitas had no interest in challenging these brutes. To suffocate in the hold was still preferable to being fed to the sharks.

Throughout the day-and-a-half-long voyage, the Benitas neither ate nor drank. The ship's food was not kosher and although they were surrounded by wooden crates and sacks of vegetables and fruit, the idea of helping themselves to the property of others was unthinkable.

JEWISH AGENCY representatives met the boat at Marseilles and, after some minor bureaucratic paperwork, led the family to a waiting bus. They were driven to Camp Aranas, an old and sparsely arranged military base with several wooden tin-roofed barracks and not much else. Rumor had it that this camp was used to house Jews for different purposes during World War II.

But nothing could dim the family's high spirits now — they were out of Africa at last and they were in the company of hundreds of Jews like themselves, refugees from Algeria, Tunisia and Libya. And most thrilling of all — they were on the threshold of a new and glorious life in *Eretz Yisrael*. Their first *Shabbat* at Camp Aranas was a beautiful, joyous celebration and a time for the camp residents to exchange chilling tales of escape.

The weather, however, was even more chilling, with temperatures plunging far below freezing. One of Eliezer's children came down with influenza, and there were no medical facilities or doctors in the camp. Eliezer was beside himself with worry.

Abu-Yosef walked through the snow to visit his cousin's barracks and offer whatever comfort he could. Inside the thin-walled bunk it was almost as bitterly cold as outside. The primitive wood-burning stove gave off more smoke than heat and the little boy coughed weakly and shivered uncontrollably. "May God bring him a speedy recovery," Abu-Yosef wished Eliezer, but the words brought no solace.

Ignoring the warnings of the camp's staff, Eliezer left the stove going that night — for the sake of the ailing, fever-wracked child — and stuffed newspaper in the cracks around the window frame to keep out the draft. Before dawn, Eliezer, his wife, his five children, and an elderly couple from Tunisia who shared their barracks, all died of asphyxiation.

ABU-YOSEF was inconsolable. After the long, grueling journey during which their lives had been in peril at every stage, his dearest friend — along with his entire family — had perished... Now Eliezer would never realize his life-long dream, and for Abu-Yosef the dream became less tantalizing. He mourned his cousin's death with a heavy, aching heart. The family looked on helplessly as Abu-Yosef aged visibly before their eyes, refusing food or drink, staring wordlessly at the bleak horizon beyond the camp.

Twelve days later, a boat arrived to take the Benitas to *Eretz Yisrael*. It was a luxury liner and the family enjoyed comforts they had never known. But Abu-Yosef was oblivious to their childlike pleasure. The pain in his heart for Eliezer had become physical and tangible, spreading to his chest and shoulders until he was hunched over from the agony of it.

ON MONDAY AFTERNOON, they docked in Haifa. The sun shone brightly and the family's joy knew no bounds. Shouting with jubilation, they ran across the gangplank and knelt to kiss the holy soil.

But Abu-Yosef lingered on the deck. Without Eliezer to share the moment of triumph, it lost all its sweetness. The family looked back with glowing faces to their father, their leader, their strength throughout the month-long ordeal, and reached out to beckon him to shore.

A force like a powerful hand at his back impelled Abu-Yosef towards them. When he stepped onto the pier, he turned his face upward to the clear blue heavens, and all at once his pain eased.

"*Baruch, shehechiyanu vekiyimanu vehigi'anu lazman hazeh.* Thank you, Lord, for having kept us alive, sustained us and enabled us to survive until this moment!"

The men who assisted the Benitas and countless other Oriental Jewish families to escape from their native lands were fellow countrymen in the employ of the Jewish Agency in Israel. Their knowledge of the terrain and familiarity with the language and customs were vital to their activity. Frequently these men delayed their own emigration by many months, and sometimes years, in order to rescue others. They must be differentiated from other employees of the Jewish Agency who processed the new immigrants upon their arrival in *Eretz Yisrael* — often with unfortunate results.

3

on Piety

הללויה שירו לד' שיר חדש
תהלתו בקהל חסידים תהלים קמט:א

✿ HalleluYah! Sing to the Lord a new song. His praise is sounded in the congregation of the pious.

Psalms 149:1

The mitzva of *tefillin* is the physical embodiment of Judaism. It signifies the intertwining of the intellect — *tefillin shel rosh* — with the emotions — *tefillin shel yad* (adjacent to the heart).

For many generations, however, it was the intellect which dominated, and Torah scholarship reigned. The emotional element was relegated to a minor role. The Baal Shem Tov, founder of Chassidism, propounded the return of emotion to a more prominent place in religious observance.

With song and story to complement study and instruction, Chassidism has penetrated countless hearts. But it was the greatness of the Chassidic *rebbes* that led to the movement's success. Their greatness lay not only in their erudition but in their gift for awakening the dormant spark of Jewishness in so many.

An Investment In The Future

ALL NIGHT LONG, the worried father paced the floor of the tiny kitchen. He stroked his beard, now flecked with grey, and paced some more. He pulled a scrap of paper from his pocket, examined it briefly, then crumpled it up and hurled it to the floor with a force born of frustration. Shivering from the cold, he wrapped his old coat more tightly over his nightshirt. He stirred the ashes in the stove, but there was little hope that the long-dead embers would glow again.

The noise hadn't disturbed Golda; she too was having a sleepless night. She joined her husband in the kitchen.

"Why don't you go see the Maggid?" she asked in her soft voice. "You wouldn't hesitate if it were a spiritual matter, so why do you hesitate for a material one?"

"You're right, Golda," her husband responded, making up his mind at last. "I'll do it. Surely we're not the only ones who can hardly make ends meet and have to bear the added expense of marrying off a daughter. The holy Maggid of Mezerich will be able to advise us — I'm certain."

And so the chassid set out on the long journey to Mezerich. There was no question that whatever suggestion or instruction the Maggid would offer, the chassid would dutifully follow. Such was his faith in the saintly Maggid.

THE MAGGID of Mezerich, Reb Dov Ber, received the chassid warmly and listened attentively to his problem. When the chassid finished unburdening himself, the Maggid said: "Here is a ruble. Take it and invest it in the first business venture you encounter."

The chassid was overwhelmed with gratitude and hurried home to his anxious wife. Armed with the precious ruble and the Maggid's blessing, he proceeded to the foremost restaurant in the commercial district, a dining establishment where all the biggest business deals were clinched. He approached a boisterous group of patrons and naively asked:

"Do you know where I can invest some money?"

"It would depend on what you're looking to buy," replied a wealthy merchant, who also happened to be one of the biggest jokers in town.

"It doesn't really matter," said the chassid, "I just want to invest."

"Well, then," the businessman said, beginning to show an interest, "how much have you got?"

"A ruble," the chassid humbly replied.

"A ruble! Ha, ha, did you hear that? The big spender wants to invest a whole ruble! Ha, ha. My World To Come, I could sell you for a ruble, but there's not much else you could buy for that price. Ha!"

The Chassid didn't waver for a moment. "I'll take it!"

"Take what?"

"Your World To Come. If you're ready to sell it for a

ruble, take this coin and let's shake on the deal. My *rebbe* instructed me to buy the first merchandise to come my way. He didn't specify further. Obviously, this was what he intended."

Thus the bargain was struck.

L ATER THAT EVENING, while the chassid and his wife were waiting for their *mazel* to change, the ruble-toting braggart related the morning's events to his own wife.

"You WHAT?!"

"That's right. The *rebbe* told him to buy the first thing that came his way — with a ruble! Can you believe it? Let me tell you, it was the easiest ruble I ever made. Like taking candy from a baby."

"How could you! Your World To Come isn't something you sell, even for a fortune!"

"Oh, be realistic. How much do you think my World To Come was worth anyway?"

"That's not the point. The point is that you must get it back! You're a businessman, you know what to do: negotiate, offer him anything, I don't care what. But *get it back!*"

His wife was so agitated that the man raced out of the house in search of the chassid. When he finally found him, he spoke with urgency: "I'm sorry, but I made a mistake. I need my World To Come back."

"Nothing doing. A bargain is a bargain. We even have witnesses."

"Here — I'll give you two rubles, I'll even give you five rubles." The man was frantic. "You see? Your *rebbe* was right — it was a terrific investment. I'm prepared to pay you a five-fold return on your money. I can assure you my World To Come isn't worth anything near five rubles — you won't get a better offer from anyone."

BUT THE CHASSID refused to give in. The Maggid had told him to invest; he hadn't said anything about selling. The merchant cajoled and pleaded, but the chassid remained adamant. Dejected, the man returned home with only the solitary ruble to show for all his efforts.

"I don't care what he said. I will not live with a man who has sold his World To Come," his wife shouted in a rage. "It is simply not something you sell! So either you move out or I move out, but I will not remain with you unless you retrieve your World To Come!"

Once again the businessman sought out the chassid to convince him to relinquish ownership. "Just name your price," he begged. "It was only meant as eh...er, as a joke. You must let me buy it back." But the chassid was unmovable in his determination to follow what he understood to be the Maggid's instructions.

Had the Maggid mentioned the option of selling, the chassid would have complied long ago. He would have done anything to stop the pestering. The situation was becoming impossible.

In exasperation the chassid suggested, "It was the Maggid who recommended that I buy something, I am only following my *rebbe*'s orders. It is not for me to decide whether or not to sell you back your World To Come — only the Maggid can decide. Let us, if you wish, travel to Mezerich and seek his advice."

AND SO the two men set off on the long trip to Mezerich, one in the hope of retrieving his World To

Come and the other in the hope of not jeopardizing the Maggid's blessing for income.

The Maggid listened patiently to the recounting of the tale and then summed it up: "So you sold your World To Come for a ruble and now wish to buy it back?"

"Yes, yes! At any price!"

"But you yourself said that your World To Come wasn't worth more than a ruble."

"Well, that's true, but now my wife's happiness depends on it, that is, on my getting it back. She will leave me if I fail. Therefore I am willing to pay anything you ask."

"All right. This chassid is about to marry off his daughter. As a man of business, you can appreciate that this is an expensive undertaking. You may buy back your World To Come, then, by paying for all the marriage expenses." He paused to await the merchant's slow but firm nod. "And in the merit of this investment," Reb Dov Ber continued, "you will have truly earned your World To Come."

Thirst

"ALLOW ME, honored *Rebbe*," began Reb Yehuda Leib MiSlonim, addressing his revered and illustrious guest, "to share a tale about a humble, simple Jew with lofty aspirations. It is a story which took place but one brief generation ago."

The *Slonimer Rebbe*, Reb Avraham, nodded to his host as he sipped the welcome glass of hot tea.

"It was winter, with weather even more severe than what we are suffering now," Reb Yehuda Leib continued. A strong gust of frigid wind rattled the shutters as if to emphasize his words. "I was trudging past the *shtiebel* through the early morning snow, when suddenly I heard a mournful voice from within that seemed to pierce the very rooftop and ascend to the heavens.

"My curiosity overcame me and I rushed inside to find the source. The shul was empty except for Ephraim Shmutzkez: the simplest Jew of all. Wrapped in his ragged overcoat, he stood before the open *aron kodesh* entreating with all his heart: 'My soul thirsts for Thee; my flesh yearns for Thee!' *(Psalms 63:3)*

"At first I was astounded. How does Ephraim come to

such words and such passion, to depths of emotion reserved for the loftiest of souls? He must be having an hallucination, I thought to myself, a wild dream. He must think himself a saint!

"I wanted to stop him, but controlled myself. I decided to wait and see what would happen for he was, as yet, unaware of my presence. It wasn't until an hour later that Ephraim ended his recital.

"With his spirits apparently restored, he began to meditate. And all the while I was wonderstruck that on an ordinary weekday Ephraim Shmutzkez could intone 'My soul thirsts for Thee' with such pathos!

"He then opened his tearful eyes and gazed at the *aron kodesh*. All at once he seemed to remember why he had come to the shul. '*Ribbono Shel Olam*,' he cried with fervor. '*Du vaist doch!* You know so well...' and began to unburden his sorrows, praying for a speedy salvation.

"**W**HAT WERE his sorrows? In order to earn enough money during those troubled economic times, Ephraim supplemented his meager income by clandestinely producing wine and liquor, circumventing the authorities and avoiding payment of taxes. The well-concealed sub-cellar under his basement had been converted into a modest distillery.

"The day before, a vindictive neighbor — perhaps a competitor — informed the authorities of Ephraim's illicit activities. A friend of Shmutzkez, who happened to be present, ran to him with the news that the informer and the Tax Collector were on their way to search the cellar! Ephraim knew his arrest was imminent.

"Shmutzkez got up and ran. To where? To the *shtiebel* to say *Tehillim* and pray for help. But when he came to the verse, 'My soul thirsts for Thee,' he forgot all that had befallen him and begged only for closeness to God."

Reb Yehuda Leib paused in his retelling and exclaimed: "Look! Look how a simple Jew, the simplest of the simple, behaved just one generation ago! The greatest of dangers was about to strike: he was to be deprived of his income, incarcerated for a serious crime, and would endure other unknown punishments and degradations. With the trouble just around the corner, did he look for any avenues of escape as most people would? Did he run to the *shtadlanim* or intermediaries, or try to bribe officials? No. It was clear to him that the only thing to do at a time like this was to run to the *aron kodesh*, say *kapitlach Tehillim* and seek Divine help.

"And not only this! After it became clear to him that this was his only hope, he opened up the *sefer Tehillim* and forgot what he was doing. He pleaded not for salvation, but for closeness to God: 'My soul thirsts for Thee; my flesh yearns for Thee!' " Reb Yehuda Leib resumed his story, adding, "You know the Almighty can do all — I wish only to relate how the story unfolded.

"**W**HILE EPHRAIM was engaged in this spiritual pursuit, his poor wife was concerned with an altogether different type of pursuit. Certain that her husband had gone to find character witnesses and advocates to plead his case, or if need be, bribe the officials, she believed he must have failed in his mission for he had not come home. Through the window of their house, she saw the informer and the taxman drawing near and suddenly she had an inspiration. Quickly she spread a thick layer of straw at the snowbound entrance to the basement.

"When they reached the Shmutzkez house, the informer pointed to the cellar door and said to the official: 'Here is the illegal distillery!'

"The official's face turned flaming red. He struck the informer a forceful blow to the jaw and the man tumbled to the icy ground. 'Do you take me for a fool?' demanded the furious official. 'Everyone knows that the presence of straw inhibits fermentation. It is impossible to produce liquor in a storehouse of hay!'

"The informer, now fearing for his own safety, cowered at the Tax Collector's feet and implored, 'Officer, sir, surely they have spread out the straw as a bluff to mislead you. I beg of you: go into the cellar and see for yourself...'

"The official became more irate and kicked the informer in the chest and head. 'It's not enough that you deceived me once and forced me to come all the way out here in this freezing cold? Do you want me to look a thorough idiot searching for liquor in a basement stuffed with hay? Ach, all this cold and talk of drink has made me thirsty,' and he stormed away from the house towards the local tavern. Thus was Ephraim Shmutzkez spared a terrible fate.

"**T**HERE IS nothing remarkable about this," concluded Reb Yehuda Leib, "for do we not know that the Almighty can do all? What is amazing is the behavior of a simple Jew just one generation ago. In the throes of mortal danger he perceived that his only hope of salvation was through prayer. And then, he suddenly realized that more than God's help, he wanted His closeness..."

The Born Loser

WHEN Rabbi Levi Yitzhak MiBerdichev learned that Mendel the wealthy businessman had passed away, he sent a message to the *chevra kadisha* requesting that the funeral procession be routed past his house. Naturally, the *chevra kadisha* complied, although the Berdichever's home was considerably out of the way.

As soon as the procession reached the *Rebbe's* street, Reb Levi Yitzhak emerged from his home resplendent in his brocade *bekeshe* and high fur hat, and strode slowly behind the coffin, accompanying Mendel to his earthly resting place. The townspeople were astounded to see such honor bestowed upon the wealthy, yet unnoteworthy departed. But if the esteemed *Rebbe* deemed Mendel deserving of honor, who were they to deny it? So they all quickly donned their finery and joined the funeral procession. Every man, woman and child in Berdichev turned out to escort Mendel on this, his final journey.

After the ceremony, an elder of the town approached Reb Levi Yitzhak. "Honored *Rebbe*," he began, "we have all known Mendel for many years, but none of us can figure out why he merited such recognition."

"I, too, knew Mendel," replied the venerable *Rebbe*, "perhaps better than anyone, and let me assure you, this was a man worthy of homage. Three times he was a litigant at a *din Torah* where I presided — and he lost each time." Seeing the elder's perplexed expression, the *Rebbe* invited him to his home and recounted for him the history of "Mendel the *Gvir*."*

S OME twenty years earlier, Mendel had been visiting the marketplace when he came upon a crowd of people standing in a circle. His curiosity aroused, he tapped a bystander on the shoulder, and the crowd — recognizing the important personage — parted to make way for him. Mendel stepped forward to see what had attracted their avid attention and there, on the ground, writhing in obvious anguish and tearing his hair out, was a stranger — ranting and raving about a lost wallet.

"Excuse me, sir," Mendel said, "perhaps I can be of some help?"

"Help? Who can help me? *Oiy, oiy*, it's gone. I'm finished! I'm broke! My life savings... *Oiy, oiy*... ten thousand rubles, ten thousand beautiful rubles — gone!"

"Can you tell me what your wallet looked like?"

"*Oiy*, what difference does it make? It's gone. I'm done for! Six daughters to marry off — with what?"

"Just describe the wallet, if you please."

---

* The term is used to describe a man of substantial means.

"*Oiy*, leave me be! Can't you see I've been wiped out? *Oiy*, all I wanted was to wheel and deal a little, be able to double my money, maybe. Marry my daughters to *bnei* Torah — and now? Nothing. They'll be spinsters! My family will starve — because I was so foolish as to lose that wretched old wallet."

"Come, come, my good man. Describe the wallet."

"All right. It was brown leather with a scratch on the right side and a brass button closure. I had ten thousand rubles in it — my life savings! I counted and recounted the money so many times I can even tell you the denominations of the notes and coins!" And he did. "But what use is it? I'll never see that money again. *Oiy, oiy!*"

"Well, I have some good news for you. I found your wallet."

"Oh, let me be," the man cried. "I'm in no mood for jokes. Have you no pity?"

"I'm not joking. My name is Mendel — anyone in town can vouch for my integrity. Here is my address. If you will be so kind as to come to my house this evening, it will be my pleasure to return your property."

THE STRANGER rose slowly to his feet. "You're, you're not fooling, then? You really found my money?"

"Yes, yes. Now pull yourself together and I'll see you around six o'clock."

The change that came over the stranger was total: gone were his tears and his distraught countenance, replaced by smiles and glowing cheeks. He danced a jig in celebration and looked skyward, shouting, "I'm saved, I'm saved!"

That evening, at precisely six o'clock, the stranger knocked on the door of Mendel's mansion and Mendel himself — wearing his superbly tailored silk caftan and matching yarmulka — answered the door. He ushered the man into his parlor and handed him the wallet.

THE MAN'S FACE gleamed as he examined the wallet and carefully counted its contents: "... nine thousand, nine thousand five hundred, ten thousand — yes, it's all here. Thank you, thank you. You're a prince, a true gentleman, a man of integ... wait a minute! This isn't my wallet — my wallet had a scratch on the right side and this one has a scratch on the left."

"Left, right — what's the difference. Of course it's your wallet."

"Hold on there, what kind of trick is this? I know my wallet and this is *not it!* I don't need charity — these ten fingers earned the ten thousand rubles; they'll earn them again."

"Look, sir, this is obviously your wallet, just as you described it, right? And the money inside is in exactly the denominations you described, right? So why don't you just take it and we'll say goodnight, hmm?"

"Oh no, you don't. If you think you're going to go to *Gan Aiden* on my *plaitzes* [Heaven on my shoulders], you've got another think coming!"

"I insist you take your wallet and that's final."

"In that case, *I* insist we go to a *din Torah.*"

The two appeared before Reb Levi Yitzhak, who listened patiently to their grievance. At last he said: "I'm sorry Mendel, but you've lost. This man is right. It is most praiseworthy that you should wish to perform the mitzva of *hashavas aveida* — returning lost property, but if the gentleman denies that the wallet *is* his property, there is nothing you can do. But," he added, placing one hand upon his heart and the other on Mendel's shoulder, "I assure you, you will be rewarded for your desire to observe the mitzva and to assist your fellow man."

THE *REBBE* paused in his narration and the elder, who by now was completely enthralled, urged him to relate the second incident. Reb Levi Yitzhak continued.

Some time later, a man from the next town asked Mendel for a loan. "I'm a merchant," he said, "and I've had many successful ventures, but lately I've suffered several reversals and I need fifteen thousand rubles to stay afloat."

"Fifteen thousand is a tidy sum. Do you have a guarantor?"

The man looked heavenward and said: "*He* is my guarantor."

"Say no more," Mendel replied, "there *is* no better assurance," and he handed the merchant fifteen thousand rubles.

Four years passed before the merchant returned. "Here is the fifteen thousand you loaned me. Thank God, it really got me back on my feet."

"Who are you, sir?" asked Mendel. "Do I know you?"

"Have you forgotten? I borrowed fifteen thousand rubles from you four years ago..."

"Ah, yes, I recall now. But the loan has long-since been repaid."

"What?!"

"Yes, of course. Your guarantor paid it."

"What do you mean, 'my guarantor paid it'?"

"When you did not return after thirty days, I applied to your guarantor and He reimbursed me."

"What are you talking about?"

"You see that building across the street? Well, He helped me build it and I have therefore been amply recompensed. Now, if you will excuse me, I'm a busy man..."

"Now wait just a minute! You can't turn to my guarantor unless I instruct you to do so. If you think you're going to go to *Gan Aiden* on my *plaitzes*, you're mistaken! I was in pretty bad shape four years ago, but I'm on my feet now — I don't have to take charity!"

"Look here," said Mendel, "I don't have time for nonsense. The loan has been repaid and that's that. If you like, we can go to a *din Torah*."

AND so they did. The *Rebbe* listened attentively to the details of their dispute and at last he said, "I'm sorry, Mendel, but you lose again. You cannot turn to the debtor's guarantor unless you appeal to the debtor first. That's the law."

"But a normal loan agreement elapses after thirty days and I waited thirty days..."

"Mendel," the *Rebbe* said, "the law is the law. Paying back a loan is a mitzva which you may not deny the borrower. But," he added, gently placing one hand on his heart and the other on Mendel's shoulder, "I personally assure you that in the merit of the mitzva you were so anxious to perform — helping out this merchant's family when they were in need — you will be justly rewarded and will receive the honor due you."

❀

THE ELDER, obviously moved by the *Rebbe*'s account of Mendel the *Gvir*'s 'misfortune,' asked: "And what, revered *Rebbe*, was the nature of the third *din Torah?*"

"This case concerned a man from right here in this town," the *Rebbe* began, "someone with whom you yourself may be acquainted..."

It was an incident which involved a man who was desperately impoverished. He and his wife and eleven children lived in a dilapidated hovel with a leaking roof and crumbling walls. They had almost nothing to eat and little prospect of improving their situation. One day the man surprised his wife by saying:

"I'm going to go to *vu der feffer vakst* [where the wild peppers grow, *i.e.*, to a distant town] — maybe there my fortune will change. You know what they say, 'Change your spot — change your lot'..."

"What?!" cried his wife in despair, "you're going to abandon us? What will become of me — I'll be an *aguna* with eleven children to raise all alone!" She flew into a rage. "How dare you think of leaving!"

AWEEK LATER, her husband visited everyone he knew in town and borrowed a little money from each — a ruble here, a half-ruble there, until at last he had amassed a grand total of thirty rubles. When he returned home, he displayed the money triumphantly and declared:

"You see this? It's only the beginning. I got a job working for Mendel the *Gvir* — out there *vu der feffer vakst* — and every week he'll pay you my salary of thirty rubles." So desperate was he to try his *mazel* somewhere else that he hoped this deception would convince her to relent and agree to his move.

She was ecstatic. In her mind she was already having the leaking roof fixed, stocking the pantry with food, and buying a dress for the little one. His wife appeased, the poor man set off for *vu der feffer vakst.*

B Y THE FOLLOWING Friday, however, the thirty rubles were gone and the wife waited expectantly for the next installment. But the money, of course, did not arrive.

Irate, she threw on her coat and marched off to the *Gvir*'s office. She stormed in and demanded to see Mendel.

"I'm sorry, Madam," said Mendel's secretary, "my employer will not see you without an appointment."

"*Your* employer is also my *husband*'s employer and he owes me thirty rubles. Now pay up!" she shouted hysterically.

"I don't know who you are, Madam, but if you wish, I can make an appointment for you for next week. But I'm afraid you'll have to leave now."

"I'm not leaving until that big boss of yours pays me!" she yelled, stamping her foot.

The secretary examined his books but could find no record of her husband on the payroll.

"I don't care what's written in your books," she screamed, "my husband is slaving away for that crook and he's going to pay me *or else!*"

HEARING THE COMMOTION in the reception room, Mendel stepped out of his office to see what was going on. "What's the trouble here?" he asked.

"You sent my husband all the way out *vu der feffer vakst* and he's working his fingers to the bone. You're supposed to be paying me his thirty-ruble-a-week salary. Now, where's the money?"

Noting her ragged cloak and agitated state, Mendel said, "Please forgive my forgetfulness. It was a terrible oversight. Here is your thirty rubles and I promise you I shall not be tardy again with the payments. I will see to it that you'll not be bothered to come here again. The money will be delivered to you promptly every Friday morning."

The woman gratefully received the money, and flounced out past the astonished secretary with an expression on her face that said, "*I told you so!*" And every week, true to his promise, Mendel sent her thirty rubles.

FIVE YEARS passed. The man who had gone to *vu der feffer vakst* had indeed succeeded in changing his *mazel* — so much so, that when he returned to town it was in an elegant carriage. His clothes, no longer rags, were exquisitely tailored of the finest silks. As the carriage drew up to his house, the man wondered with trepidation at the reception his wife would give him.

He hadn't corresponded with her at all during the entire five years. Was she still alive? How had she managed all this time? What had become of his eleven children? He was filled with remorse over his unforgivable neglect and terrified at the prospect of facing his wife's fury. He could only hope that the fortune he had made would somehow recompense her for the years of suffering.

But the sight that greeted him when he stepped down from the carriage made him rub his eyes in disbelief. The ramshackle hovel was completely refurbished, freshly painted and with a new roof and shutters. The yard was immaculate, blooming with flowers and surrounded by a neat white fence. And seated on a bench was the *melamed,* teaching his youngest son — and *smiling,* as though he'd been recently paid. The man had never seen the *melamed* smile before.

Through the window he could see his wife working in the kitchen, baking cakes and cooking what smelled like a sumptuous meal. She noticed him at that moment and ran out to greet him.

"You were right, after all. Our *mazel* did change and your employer, Mendel the *Gvir,* was completely reliable. Every week like clockwork he delivered your salary — thirty rubles, just like you said. We even have a little money put aside now for our daughters' dowries."

T HE MAN was appalled and could hardly wait until morning to return the vast sum of money he owed to Mendel. Directly after *davening* he sped to the office of the *Gvir* — cash in hand.

"I don't know how to thank you for all you've done," he said to Mendel, "but I am a wealthy man in my own right now and wish to return the money. Here is the entire amount you paid my wife — I figured it out: thirty rubles a week for five years."

"I'm afraid I don't know who you are," said Mendel, "and you've caught me just at the start of a business day. I hope you'll excuse me..."

"I'm the man whose wife and family you've been supporting for the last five years."

"I don't know what you're talking about, and like I said — I'm very busy!"

"**Y**OU CAN'T fool me! You know that you have sustained my family all this time and now you must take back all of the money."

"No, no," Mendel protested, "I only paid the salary your wife claimed I owed. I will not take any money from you."

"Now see here. I was poverty-stricken five years ago and I only made up the story about being in your employ so that my wife would let me leave for a distant city where the opportunities were better. Well, I made my fortune and now I insist you allow me to repay you."

But Mendel wouldn't hear of it. "You'll have to excuse me. I'm a busy man..."

"What do you mean?" The man was furious. "I don't need charity! You think you'll go to *Gan Aiden* on my *plaitzes*? No, sir! Let's see what the *Rebbe* has to say."

AND SO Mendel appeared once again before the Berdichever for a *din Torah*. The *Rebbe* heard the two men out and this time Mendel fought for his case as if his life depended on it, but the *Rebbe* didn't hesitate for a moment with his decision.

"Mendel, my friend, you're a born loser. This is the third time you've come before me and for the third time I must tell you that you have lost. But, believe me," he said, placing one hand on his heart and the other on Mendel's shoulder, "you will receive full credit for the mitzva of supporting this man's family, for maintaining *shalom bayis* in his household, and for providing dowries for his daughters."

Finally, the elder understood why unremarkable Mendel the *Gvir*, the wealthiest man in town, had earned the greatest honor. The "Born Loser" had won at last.

☗ There is another version of this story in which "Mendel the *Gvir*" is reputed to be the town miser. The townspeople are therefore astonished that such a tight-fisted individual should merit the great honor of having the pious and saintly Reb Levi Yitzhak attend his funeral. The *Rebbe* explains that Mendel had three *din Torah*s at which he presided — and *won* them all.

on Faith

הנה עפלה לא ישרה נפשו בו
וצדיק באמונתו יחיה חבקוק ב:ד

*Behold, his soul is puffed up;
it is not upright in him — but the
righteous shall live by his faith.*

Habbakuk 2:4

"The foundation of foundations and pillar of wisdom," writes the Rambam, "is to know that there is a primordial Creation." It is that *knowledge* — not supposition, not belief, not assumption — that is profound in significance.

"Knowing" indicates a certainty so absolute that one may stake his life on it. Such, contends the Rambam, is the level of faith a Jew must have — for this is the foundation of the Torah.

But while such total confidence in the Almighty's omnipotence is the "pillar of wisdom," it is often the most simple and unsophisticated among us who possess it.

Lord vs. Landlord:
No Contest

THE BRONX. Once the respectable "uptown" address of successful Jewish immigrants of earlier years, it was, in the 1960s, still home to ninety thousand of them. The stately mansions all along the Grand Concourse had been subdivided and converted into three-, four- and five-room apartments where the Jewish population continued to live in relative harmony in that huge ethnic melting pot. They would stroll on Pelham Parkway, read the newspapers in the park or discuss the Workmen's Circle on the stoop. There were more *Forwards* delivered to the corner candy store than copies of *The Daily News*. True, the Bronx was Jewish, but it wasn't particularly religious.

IN THE MIDDLE of all this was the Wallace Avenue Shul, a little hideaway for old men who cherished the warmth of the bare *shtiebel*, a place where they could hold on to their past. The Rabbi was Yisrael Rabinowitz, a pudgy, good humored Jew from Lomza who had survived the Poles, the Germans and the Russians — which made it likely that he would survive the Americans too.

The Wallace Avenue Shul and its rabbi didn't look like much, but everyone knew they enjoyed the special Grace of God. For Rabbi Rabinowitz the shul was home, and there he would learn Torah from four-thirty in the morning until ten o'clock at night. One morning, his predawn entry into the shul foiled the plans of two thieves who were engaged at that moment in breaking a hole through the shul wall into the Orlinsky supermarket next door. More about that wall — and the supermarket — later.

ANOTHER WALL of the synagogue, shared with an adjacent bakery, was known as the *"haise vant"* because of the oven mounted on the bakery side. One Friday afternoon, a large volume of gas had accumulated in the oven. When the pilot was lit later that night, the oven exploded with a force which ripped through the ceiling. It generated a blaze the likes of which the Bronx hadn't known for years.

Two city blocks of Wallace/Lydig Avenue were engulfed in a four-alarm fire that raged through nine stores. Looking down the street that night observers saw a hook-and-ladder truck every ten yards and scores of grim-faced firefighters directing hoses and opening hydrants. And there was Rabbi Rabinowitz, standing before his shul, *Tehillim* in hand, praying in the glow of the fire. The next morning every Italian, Black, Puerto Rican and who-knows-what from the neighborhood filed through the synagogue during Shabbos services to see with his own eyes the shul that hadn't burnt down.

EVERY FRIDAY Rabbi Rabinowitz telephoned an employment agency to send someone to mop the shul's floor. By the late 'sixties the Bronx had already justly earned its reputation as a jungle, and it was the "natives of the wild" who were sent for the job. But Rabbi Rabinowitz was undaunted. Back in Lomza, and later in Siberia, he had lived through worse. Actually his background provided the necessary skills for dealing with indigenous populations: his offers of hot coffee and an occasional free meal were met with surprise and appreciation. His kind words in pidgin English brought out the best in all who passed through.

One Sunday afternoon on his way back from a *simcha* on the Lower East Side, Rabbi Rabinowitz was accosted by six thugs. "Hey," yelled one of the muggers, "ain't ya dat Ray-bye from up dere in de Bronx? Let him go, guys. He's ma Man." The group dissolved, and the astonished rabbi resumed breathing.

The rampant crime which pervaded the Bronx compelled the Wallace Avenue Shul — per order of the Police Commissioner — to install a "buzzer lock." Soon after it was in operation, a member complained to the rabbi that he had knocked one evening but the door wasn't buzzed open. Rabbi Rabinowitz, reasoning that the shul and its rabbi were obligated above all to serve the community, decided to forget about the buzzer, and the door remained open from then on (a noble gesture, to be sure, but one fraught with hazard).

Hoodlums who frequented the Carvel Ice Cream store across the street liked to impress their girlfriends by throwing lit firecrackers and cherry bombs through the open shul door. On one occasion, two teenagers heaved a can of garbage inside. They had the misfortune of having it land on a policeman who had come in to pay "*yizkor* money." The officer chased after the "poipetratas," apprehended them, and administered a little justice of his own before he brought them before the due offices of the law to administer its own fair share. Word of this incident spread quickly through the neighborhood and quiet reigned for a while at the Wallace Avenue Shul.

I N FACT, the only major problem which plagued the shul was the neighboring supermarket's persistent drive to expand to house a meat department. Such an expansion was, in the eyes of many *baalei batim*, a godsend for the shul. According to Orlinsky's plan, the shul — which was too large to begin with — would be divided in half, thus cutting the rent, heating, cleaning and lighting bills. The landlord of both properties, aching to expand the supermarket because of the potential jump in revenue, even sweetened the pot by offering the shul a long-dreamed-of lease. But Rabbi Rabinowitz wouldn't hear of it. "What! Turn a shul into a *treifa* butcher shop, open on Shabbos?!"

He took his case everywhere but he didn't stand a chance. He even appealed to State Senator Samuel Bernstein and Borough President Robert Abrams, who offered their sympathy but explained that without a lease there was nothing that could be done.

I N THE MEANTIME, the landlord resorted to other means of persuasion. He had a whole bag of dirty tricks: He paid welfare recipients to make threatening phone calls, and when that failed, he arranged for a phony city inspector to examine the shul.

In marched the landlord and the inspector — actually a cashier from the supermarket next door disguised in a white cloak with a shiny, official-looking badge (bought for a dime in a toy store). To start with, he told the rabbi that the floor wasn't safe and called for his "assistants" waiting outside. Instantly, a crew appeared hauling planks and demolition equipment. The "inspector" then turned his attention to the wall separating the supermarket from the shul. "This wall is no good," he declared and with the help of his eager workers started pulling away the sheetrock.

Rabbi Rabinowitz finally sensed that something wasn't kosher and telephoned Mr. Friedman, a congregant better versed in English and less naive than himself. As soon as Mr. Friedman sized up the situation, he threatened to call the police. The "inspector" fled.

After this tactic had also failed, the landlord raised the rent from $200 to $1,000 a month, a sum way beyond the shul's meager means. The landlord wasted no time in filing a suit against the shul for "refusing" to pay the rent. As *mazel* and Rabbi Rabinowitz would have it, the judge was a devout Catholic: His Honor threw the landlord out of court for ruthless treatment of a house of worship.

But the landlord still was unwilling to forego the higher rent of the supermarket, which threatened to relocate if it couldn't expand. He appealed the decision of the lower court to the New York Court of Appeals. This time it seemed hopeless for Rabbi Rabinowitz; even the shul members were on the side of the landlord who promised to lower the original rent and give them "whatever they want" as long as the store could enlarge.

The court hearing was set for a Tuesday. The previous week Rabbi Rabinowitz visited all of the prominent rabbis and *roshei yeshiva* for blessings. Even some of the *rebbes* failed to see the significance of the issue — but Rabbi Rabinowitz was unshakeable.

THAT SUNDAY afternoon Lydig Avenue was suddenly startled by a loud crashing sound emanating from Orlinsky's supermarket. With no apparent cause, the store's roof had caved in. Since it was Sunday, no one was inside. Since it happened during the afternoon, half the Bronx was on hand to witness the omen.

The next morning the Fire Commissioner was

astonished to discover that the shul was intact. "Rabbi," he began, removing his cap, "er, excuse me for disturbing you while you're studying, but maybe you know what happened here? How could it be that the supermarket is totally demolished and your temple didn't lose a chip of paint? I hear they've been giving you some trouble...? Well, there you have it — an Act of God."

The only one unaffected by the miracle was the landlord. He informed the rabbi, in no uncertain terms, that he intended to pursue his case.

On Tuesday morning, the day of the court case, the landlord received a phone call from the Emergency Ward at Jacobi Hospital informing him that his daughter had been injured in a car accident. Before he left for the hospital, he made one important call:

"O.K., Rabbi, I give in — you can keep your shul..."

The Kugel Carriage

REB USHER was the tragicomic figure of the Mirrer Yeshiva in Jerusalem, but there was really very little comical about him.

How he survived the death camps was a mystery, but he served as a constant reminder of the living casualties of the war. Bowlegged, with a perpetually craned neck, he clearly had lost some of his senses in the Nazi inferno. His home was a tiny Meah Shearim hovel, but most of the time he lived in the Mirrer Yeshiva.

Yes, he truly lived there, or more precisely, on the third bench from the back on the right side of the *beis midrash*. The third bench was Reb Usher's bed and home which he shared with the Yeshiva during the *sedarim*. Every once in a while he would attempt some small repair in the *beis midrash* or drive in a loose nail. It was his way of paying the rent.

Reb Usher didn't have a closet. Nor did he need one. He owned nothing more than the clothes on his back — except for his one prized possession. His pride, the only thing in the world that belonged to him, was a broken down baby carriage. Every night he parked his carriage on the ground floor of the Yeshiva, and until it was securely stowed away he wouldn't head upstairs to the *beis midrash* to retire.

How Reb Usher cherished that battered buggy! If someone would ever fiddle or tamper with it he would make a fuss and commotion that could be heard throughout the entire neighborhood. One day a boy tried to remove a teething ring that was dangling from the tattered hood, and Reb Usher screamed as if mortally wounded.

The baby carriage was the sole means of Reb Usher's income. His profession: *kugel shlepping.* All Friday and Shabbos* Reb Usher could be seen delivering his cargo with great pride and joy, all over Jerusalem.

On Shabbos Reb Usher was king. He dispensed not just kugel, but blessings as well: "Reb Chaim, may you be *zocheh* to make an *aufruf* next Shabbos." "Reb Yisrael Yankov — *a sach nachas* — may the Almighty allow me to bring you a kugel next year for another *kiddush.*"

Reb Usher delivered his kugels to *roshei yeshiva* and *rebbes* in a route which stretched from Meah Shearim to Mattersdorf. "They're all my friends and customers," he boasted. "No one can make a *simcha* without Reb Usher." He even delivered a kugel to Menachem Begin after he was elected Prime Minister. "He wished me 'good Shabbos' in Yiddish," Reb Usher related.

L ATE ONE SHABBOS as Reb Usher was returning from a delivery near Davidka Square, a chassid told him that the *eiruv* around Jerusalem was broken. Reb Usher thought for a second, and then abandoned his carriage in the middle of the street. He marked the spot carefully in his mind and walked home "all alone" to the Mirrer Yeshiva.

* The presence of an *eiruv* (enclosure — *Orach Chaim* 341-54) surrounding Jerusalem enables one to carry there on Shabbos.

As soon as Shabbos was over he sent some Yeshiva students to the Davidka to retrieve his precious buggy — but it was gone! They searched frantically, knowing full well the tragic repercussions of returning to the Yeshiva without it. Local residents they questioned couldn't offer a clue as to its whereabouts.

Nervous and despondent about the anguish they were certain their news would bring, the boys returned to the Yeshiva empty-handed. Reb Usher was waiting for them at the door. The oldest among them stammered and mumbled until he mustered the courage to break the news he had rehearsed.

BEFORE THE WORDS could even sink in, Reb Usher looked towards Heaven and said, "*Der Aibershter,* the Almighty has taken away my baby carriage. He will return my baby carriage." And with that, Reb Usher seemed to dismiss the entire incident.

His behavior was inexplicable. The *bochurim* at the Yeshiva spoke of little else all week, and took up a collection to buy a new carriage for the "kugel-shlepper." Yet all this time Reb Usher continued to act as though nothing was out of order. His faith was astounding.

On Friday, as the students were planning to make their purchase, they noticed Reb Usher heading purposefully toward Davidka Square. Following him at a distance, they saw him approach the square... and find his carriage — exactly where he had left it.

The Gunner of
Tzavarone

THE CREWMEN of tank One 'B', unit code name: *Tzavarone*, had been together a long time. Nearly five years in fact, in the *beis midrash* and on the battlefield, and this summer was to be their final · tour of duty before completing obligatory army service. More than mere soldiers assigned at random to the same combat unit, they were friends and partners in learning, and considered themselves fortunate to have such comrades-in-arms.

Yes, they were a close-knit group — except for the new gunner. An ardent kibbutznik of the "HaShomer HaTzair" variety, the gunner was the proverbial thorn in their side. He never missed an opportunity to spout the virulent anti-religious "Young Guard" ideology he so zealously espoused.

The *hesder* boys had classified him as a *tinok shenishba,* a Jew raised without benefit of Jewish education or identity, and viewed him more with pity than contempt. Despite this issue, however, the gunner knew his job well; on the battlefield, petty differences were put aside and the tank crew worked as a team should. They had no alternative.

ON JUNE 11, 1982, a few days into Operation Peace for Galilee, tank One 'B', unit code name: *Tzavarone* was put to the test. Leading the advance northward on Sultan Yakub, the tank unit climbed steadily toward Hamra, a town perched atop a hill overlooking the Bekaa Valley. Hamra's hill resembles a sharply-bent knee, so that almost before tank One 'B' had traversed the crest, it had begun its descent. Waiting below were twelve Syrian tanks setting the crosshairs of their gunsights on their unsuspecting guests.

Sight met sight. The Israeli commander slammed the hatch closed and ordered his crew to commence firing. The loader fed shells into the cannons as rapidly as was humanly possible. The gunner fired; the driver reversed; and the commander radioed to the rest of the unit that they were caught in an enemy ambush. At a range of two kilometers, it takes a tank no more than forty seconds to knock out an enemy target. Accordingly, it should take twelve tanks no more than three-point-three seconds to do the job.

The Israelis immediately destroyed three Syrian tanks, but the situation remained hopeless. A tank can defend itself only through concealment or by offense. For One 'B', concealment lay nine hundred meters uphill, and forty-two tons of armor crawling and sliding up rocky terrain is anything but agile. Offensive capability is limited by reality.

ROUNDS OF 155 and 175 millimeter artillery shells, fired from batteries deep inside the Bekaa, began to pour. Although artillery fired from that distance isn't likely to score a direct hit, the deadly shrapnel showers it generates preclude bailing out.

Trapped inside little more than a square meter of steel, the crewmen made the most of their three-point-three seconds. It was a blistering hundred and twenty degrees inside the tank and the smell of sweat and gunpowder made tongues and eyes smart. The gunner tried in vain to see through sights clouded by smoke and whirling sand, while the commander emptied machinegun cartridges into the air — an exercise in futility. IDF soldiers are trained: when there is no way out, shoot until the end.

I T PROBABLY didn't take more than fifteen seconds until they were hit. A shell slammed into the left tread, hurling the tank two and a half meters into the air. The commander opened the hatch to check for fire. The greatest fear of a tank crew is that of being roasted alive in their sealed vehicle. At the first sign of flames, they would have fled, no matter what the odds.

The tank was not ablaze, but the gunner couldn't resume firing for shrapnel had jammed the turret muzzle. The driver also couldn't resume his retreat, for with one tread paralyzed, the more pressure he applied to the accelerator pedal, the faster the tank spun in a circle.

The situation deteriorated from desperate to irreversible — to despair. Shells landed in dizzying succession; nine Syrian tanks fired unremittingly while One 'B' writhed in helpless circles like a great beast mortally wounded. The end was upon them... What was there left to do?

At that moment, the *Shomer HaTzair* gunner threw his hands up and cried: "*Shema Yisrael,* I don't know the rest! *Shema Yisrael,* I don't know the rest...!"

WHILE HIS WORDS still echoed in the confined space, an altogether different sound was heard: Clangg! A giant hook heaved from the Israeli side of the hill landed on their tank and found purchase between the stowage rack and the engine louvres. The cable became taut and began to tow, gained momentum, and swiftly extricated *Tzavarone* and its crew from the claws of death.

3
on Integrity

תתן אמת ליעקב חסד לאברהם
אשר נשבעת לאבֹתינו מימי קדם

מיכה ז:כ

❀You will provide truth to
Yaakov, kindness to Avraham,
as You have sworn to our
fathers from days of old.

Micah 7:20

The term "integrity" denotes
completeness, the quality of being whole. It
also expresses rectitude and honesty. To a
Jew, the two connotations are one, for
without honesty, he is not complete.

Ironically, that very attribute which would
make us whole, may also deprive us of
tranquility. Rabbi Mendel of Kotsk, the
chassidic *rebbe* who devoted his life to truth,
taught that "a life in quest of truth is a life of
struggle in which peace and easily-won
comforts have no part." Is this, then; the fate
of the truth-seeker, to suffer perennial
turmoil for his pursuit of integrity?

Fortunate is the generation graced with
luminaries whose lofty personal standards of
honesty demonstrate that inner tranquility is
the reward — not the price — of truth.

To Bruck
Or Not To Bruck

THERE ARE three ways to identify a Litvak: the Slow Way, the Quick Way, and the Sure Way.

According to the "Slow Way," one must first strike up an acquaintance, and get to know the person. The Litvak will soon reveal his incisive, analytical bent of mind — an attribute on which he prides himself. Likewise, with time, one may discern a slight aloofness of nature.

The "Quick Way" — more direct — is by simply listening to his pronunciation, e.g.: "Torah" in Galician dialect is *Toy-ruh,* whereas in Lithuanian dialect it is *Tay-reh.* "Fish un Fleish" becomes *Fiss un Fleiss.* There is evidence as well in his liturgy: does he say *Hodu* or *Baruch Sheamar?* Does he say *Kegavna* or *Ba'me Madlikin?*

It should be borne in mind, though, that the above methods are inconclusive. The one "Sure Way" of identifying a Litvak is by observing his custom on Passover: a Litvak worthy of the name eats *gebrochts.** It's practically

---

* Because of uncertainty if all the flour in a matza is thoroughly baked, some refrain from allowing matza to come in contact with water, which might cause the unbaked flour to leaven. Such moistened matza is referred to as "gebrochts."

a matter of principle. Any Litvak who does *not* eat *gebrochts* is clearly an imposter.

IT IS ALL the more perplexing, then, that Reb Yaakov Kamenetsky, the *gaon* of Lithuanian Jewry, abstains from this tradition of his fellow countrymen, even on the last day of *Pesach*, when many chassidim are inclined to indulge. The explanation has nothing to do with genealogy but rather with Reb Yaakov's conception of honesty.

As a young teenager, Reb Yaakov, like the other yeshiva *bochurim* in Slobodka, ate *teg* — "daily" meals at the homes of various *baalei batim*. The students in almost every case were dependent upon the generosity of these householders for sustenance and could therefore ill afford to be too selective.

ONE PASSOVER, Reb Yaakov received an invitation to a home where the standard of kashrus was questionable. When he realized that the alternatives he was faced with were either to partake of a possibly "*treifa*" meal or to embarrass his hosts by refusing a gracious invitation, Reb Yaakov saw but one solution to his predicament: He informed his host that, to his profound regret, it was not his custom to eat *gebrochts* during *Pesach*.

So that this statement, entirely legitimate within the framework of "the ways of peace," should not be construed as a falsehood, Reb Yaakov resolved from that moment on never to eat *gebrochts*.

The Truth Hurts

ONE EARLY MORNING on his way to *cheder*, Yaakov Kamenetsky was detained by a distraught young man. "*Yingeleh*," the man pleaded, "I know you're on your way to *daven* and learn Torah, but I am in desperate need of help." The man was so distressed that Yaakov would gladly have performed any deed in order to help. As it was, the man's request was but a simple one:

"My son's bris is scheduled to take place momentarily and in my nervousness and haste I neglected to bring the baby's blanket. My guests have already arrived and it would be improper for me to leave them in order to return home now. Please, *yingeleh*, be so kind as to do this great *chessed* for me." He pressed a key into Yaakov's small hand. "My house is on Pilsudskiego Street, Number 3, and the blanket is on the kitchen table."

Happy to oblige, six-year-old Yaakov Kamenetsky accepted the key and hurried to Pilsudskiego. He made his way quickly through the narrow, winding streets of the shtetl, looking neither left nor right, intent only on the performance of the mitzva.

AT LAST, mission accomplished, he once again set off for school, but his detour caused him to arrive at *cheder* twenty minutes late. A stern-faced *rebbe* greeted him at the door.

"Where have you been all this time?" the *rebbe* demanded. Yaakov explained the delay and apologized for his tardiness.

His *rebbe*, however, was skeptical. He was convinced that Yaakov had stopped on the way to *cheder* to watch the construction work going on at a nearby building site — a temptation few of his classmates were able to resist. Angry at the child for inventing an excuse, the *rebbe* slapped Yaakov across the face!

Reb Yaakov found it difficult, even many years later, to condone his *rebbe*'s behavior. "It is essential for a *rebbe* to know his students well enough to be able to determine when — and if — they are lying. Punishing a child when he tells the truth is unforgivable..."

Post Paid

THE POSTAL SERVICE in Tzivityan, Lithuania was computerized long before the high-tech age of automated banks and electronic cash registers: it had Valinkov. Valinkov's brain was like a pocket calculator. He could add up a column of figures standing on his head and never make a mistake. Indeed, so accustomed were the townspeople to his unerring accuracy that they never even bothered to count their change.

Except once. On that fateful day Valinkov had had an argument with his wife and a Jewish customer benefited from the clerk's distraction. By chance he counted his change and discovered, to his amazement, that an error had been made in his favor.

He returned at once to the post office and said humbly to the clerk: "I'm afraid, sir, that your arithmetic was wrong."

Valinkov was irate, offended by the affront to his impeccable reputation, and quickly whipped out a fresh sheet of scrap paper to redo his calculations.

But no matter which way he added, the total differed from his original one. "You see?" the Jew said, "I was given fifteen kopecks extra," and he placed a handful of coins on the counter and left.

THE CLERK was speechless. *No one* — least of all a Jew — reimbursed the Government! Why, in those years (between the World Wars) Lithuania's Jewish population was sufficiently victimized by governmental agencies to justify grand larceny. But this? This insignificant overpayment didn't even qualify as pilfering; it was more like a gift, albeit a modest one. And who would reject a gift from the Government?

"Perhaps," thought the clerk, "that is the reason he returned the money — it was too paltry a sum to be worth the risk of being caught." Valinkov decided to test the next Jew who entered the post office, this time with a more irresistible amount. True, he would have to make up the deficit from his own pocket, but it was worth it.

Later that day, Valinkov went ahead with his plan. When the Jew discovered the discrepancy, he was tempted to remain silent and simply enjoy the Government's unexpected largesse. His conscience, however, gave him no rest. He brought his dilemma before Tzivityan's rabbi — Reb Yaakov Kamenetsky.

Reb Yaakov made his *psak* perfectly clear: a Jew is forbidden to possess even the smallest fraction of a coin that does not rightfully belong to him. Word spread swiftly throughout the town.

It was just before closing time and Valinkov had been congratulating himself on his perspicacity when the Jew walked into the post office. The bewildered clerk could do nothing but accept the proffered bundle of notes. "Can they all be so naive... or honest?" he wondered.

Again and again the clerk tested the honesty of the Jews of Tzivityan, but Reb Yaakov's firm ruling and his sterling example fortified the people and they withstood the trials.

WHEN THE Nazis marched into Tzivityan one year later, it was this Gentile clerk, and this Gentile alone, who risked his own safety to rescue the Jews of the town. They had proven themselves to be a holy people, undeserving of such a dire fate.

on Greatness

אמר רבי האי דמחדדנא מחבראי
דחזיתיה לר' מאיר מאחוריה
ואילו חזיתיה מקמיה הוה
מחדדנא טפי דכתיב : והיו עיניך
רואות את מוריך עירובין יג : (ישעיה 30:20)

Rebbi declared: the only reason why I am keener than my colleagues is that I saw the back of Reb Meir, but had I had a front view of him I would have been keener still, for it is written in Scriptures, '...but your eyes shall see your teacher.'

Eiruvin 13b (Isaiah 30:20)

An anthology of Jewish stories lacking adequate recognition of our great luminaries would be as meaningless as a transcription of a ship's log with no mention of its captain.

Studying the lives of the *Gedolim* does more than increase understanding of a period in history. It sheds light on the spiritual potential inherent in man. In their words and in their deeds, these men were paragons of Jewish living.

Rabbi Akiva Eiger, the leading Torah figure of his time, can truly be viewed as the mentor and *rebbe* of all succeeding generations of scholars, including Reb Berel Soloveitchik and Reb Leib Gurwicz. Their inspiring stories awaken aspirations to reach the heights of human achievement.

I Rejoice
At Your Words

I N THE YEAR 5594 (1834) Menachem Man Ream and Simcha Zimmel, partners of the Vilna-Horadna Press issued a proclamation that their firm was about to print a beautiful new *shas* with a number of additional commentaries. The printers received impressive approbations for the project from the leading rabbinic figures of the time. Among those distinguished endorsers were Rabbi Aballi Passeveller of Vilna, Rabbi Aryeh Leib of Brisk and the chief Torah authority of the generation, Rabbi Akiva Eiger. The latter also permitted them to include annotations which had been printed earlier in Prague. Together with the endorsement, a copyright was issued strictly forbidding other firms from publishing a similar *shas* for twenty years after the completion of the printing.

No sooner had this news circulated than a counterproclamation was issued by Rabbi Moshe Shapiro, the *Av Beis Din* and printer of Slavita. He had published a *shas* seventeen years before and his copyright had not yet expired. His sons, who had taken over the press, intended to print a new *shas* edition even more beautiful than the preceding one, with a copyright which would extend from this new printing for a further twenty years.

The Vilna publishers claimed that since all of the copies of the Slavita *shas* had been sold, its publisher would suffer no loss as a result of Vilna's printing, nor would it constitute an encroachment upon the prohibition of trespassing (השגת גבול). (Thus had earlier authorities ruled in favor of the Kaposit printers in their contention against the Slavita press.*)

OVER THIS seemingly niggling disagreement, the entire Jewish population of Europe was divided. The majority supported the Slavitans — not so much because they believed Slavita's claim to be just, as because of Slavita's reputation. Not only were the Shapiros righteous individuals, descendants of holy forebears such as Reb Pinchas MiKaretz, but the Slavita name guaranteed that the *sefer* would be both accurate and of the finest quality, with neither money nor effort spared in the production. The Vilna publishers, on the other hand, did not enjoy the public's trust; Vilna had never before printed classic holy books.

Nonetheless, the Vilna Press had acquired rabbinic approval, in addition to a copyright which prohibited even the Slavitans from printing a new *shas* for twenty years. They had also invested a substantial sum of money in the preparation for printing.

The Slavita Press rejected the pro-Vilna declarations of the Rabbis, claiming that although it had indeed sold all of its *shas* sets, there remained numerous individual volumes and the only way to complete these sets was by printing the *shas*

---

* כן פסק גם הג"מ ר"ז מרגליות ז"ל מבראדי ככתוב בספרו "בית אפרים" לאמור: "אחרי נמכר גאולה תהיה לו."

afresh. Furthermore, their original copyright was still valid
for three more years. To bolster their claim, they set about
acquiring new endorsements, and an extension of their
father's copyright.

Both parties entered into litigation and the three
dayanim pronounced the following compromise: the Slavita
Press would be allowed to print its *shas* but could not ban
the Vilna Press from doing so as well, since the latter had
already invested a great deal of money and secured rabbinic
support.

NEITHER SIDE accepted the compromise and each
strove to out-forbid the other. The Slavitans received
many approbations from the rabbinic authorities of
Vahleen, Galicia, Poland, Austria and, most notably, from
Rabbi Yaakov Orenstein, *Av Beis Din* of Levov and author
of *Yeshuos Yaakov*. They also acquired the support of
many chassidic *rebbes* such as Rabbi Mordechai
MiChernobel.

The Vilnaers received backing from the rabbinic
authorities of Lithuania, Zamut and Germany, including
Rabbi Yaakov Shick, the *Av Beis Din* of Karlin and author of
Mishkenos Yaakov; Rabbi Aryeh Leib Katzenelenboigen,
Av Beis Din of Brisk; Reb Akiva Eiger; his son Shlomo, *Av
Beis Din* of Kalish; and his son-in-law, Moshe Sofer — the
Chasam Sofer. Each side accumulated close to a hundred
endorsements and copyright guarantees, generating an
argument of monumental proportion and driving a wedge
between the communities of European Jewry.

The overwhelming majority of the prominent halachic
authorities were inclined to follow the opinion of Reb Akiva
Eiger and uphold the original approbation awarded to the
Vilna Press banning the printing of a new Slavita *shas*,
despite the popular support Slavita's cause enjoyed.

Many rabbis interceded to effect a compromise. The parties appeared in court a second time, but once again the *Beis Din* ruled in favor of the Vilna Press. Vilna would have the exclusive right to print the *shas* but it would be obliged to buy from the Slavita Press all of its old stock of single volumes.

The Slavitans, however, refused to stop printing their new *shas* and were furious over the stand taken by Reb Akiva Eiger and his supporters. In their bitterness over the fortune they had already invested and the profit that would be denied them (by 1836 both presses had completed printing three volumes), they derided Reb Akiva and accused his son Shlomo of accepting a bribe from the Vilna Press to solicit his father's support.

THE SLAVITANS' insults and derision were directed at Reb Akiva Eiger, but it was understood that these were tantamount to an affront to the Torah itself. Even he – a man of legendary humility – could not remain silent in the face of this *chilul Hashem*. He wrote the following letter:

> *My heart is terribly disturbed by the gall of the Slavita printers. Not only have they lied concerning my son, accusing him of having swayed my heart; but even worse they have spoken against me, accusing me of being enticed into judging a matter without first hearing from both sides, Heaven forfend!*

> *In my very endorsement for the Vilna Press I wrote specifically that I was sent all the pertinent material from the Slavita Press and nonetheless they are still trying to turn me into a liar, God forbid. Indeed I reviewed all their letters and did not find even a thousandth of a reason to justify their claim. Their entire foundation is based on the ruling of Rabbi Aballi*

*and even he did not find a case for them except for the
fact that their copyright has not yet expired. This fact
we were well aware of, but according to our Holy
Torah, the law is in accord with the Vilna Press.*

*That they wish to forcibly assert their claim I find
unforgivable. As for myself, I do not take offense, but
one may not condone a disgrace to the Torah.*

Many great rabbis were appalled at the nerve of the
Slavitans to slur Reb Akiva Eiger. Reb Shlomo Zalman
Tiktin, the *Av Beis Din* of Breslau, was one of the many who
penned letters of outrage over this insult. He concluded his
letter: למען יוסרו עושי רשעה וכו' "...that they may suffer, these
doers of iniquity."

T O COMPOUND the problem which was tearing
European Jewry asunder, an unrelated incident
occurred which brought the *shas* issue to the attention of
the authorities. A binder was dismissed from the Slavita
Press, either on the grounds of inebriation or disloyalty to
his employers. Despondent over the loss of his job and sole
source of income, he broke into the bindery one night and
hanged himself from the rafters.

The following morning, his body was discovered and a
doctor was rushed to the scene. He pronounced the binder
dead and suggested that under the circumstances it would
be best to bury him secretly. ("Enlightenists" who were
denied having their books published by the Slavita Press —
which printed only *sifrei kodesh* — were known to vent their
wrath on the ears of the Government.) But the secret was
quickly uncovered.

Relatives of the deceased and opponents of the Slavita
Press notified the police that the managers of the press had
murdered the binder and secretly buried him for

threatening to inform the authorities about books that had been published without Governmental (censor's) review. The regional governor reported to his superiors in St. Petersburg, and word of the incident even reached Czar Nikolai himself.

A team of inspectors and judges, headed by Prince Vasilchkov, was dispatched to Slavita. The investigation was slated to continue for close to a year, and for the duration, Reb Moshe Shapiro's two sons were incarcerated and their press sealed with the stamp of the Government. The Shapiro family distributed substantial sums aimed at expediting the proceedings.

The Count of Slavita was well aware of the Shapiros' integrity and revulsion for violence. He attempted to spare them from this libel and, at a gala affair he hosted to honor Prince Vasilchkov, he pleaded on behalf of his townsmen.

I N FACT, there was so much intervention on behalf of the Shapiros that their opponents were able to contend convincingly that the Shapiros had stooped to bribing even the highest ranking officials. Thus a directive was issued from St. Petersburg to have the prisoners transferred to Kiev and to rehear all the evidence there.

The brothers were led to Kiev in chains and separately placed in solitary confinement where they remained for three years, until a verdict was at last reached. They were to receive 1,500 floggings by running the gantlet three times between two rows of 250 soldiers armed with bludgeons. If they survived the blows, they would be exiled to Siberia.

When the judge read their verdict, they accepted it as God's will but were saddened by the knowledge that if they were to die at the gantlet, they would not be buried in a Jewish cemetery. This distressed them more than the prospect of death.

Just before the execution of the punishment, the judge announced that he would honor one last request. The brothers pleaded to be allowed burial in a Jewish cemetery, and the judge acquiesced. Their spirits were lifted.

O N *ROSH CHODESH ELUL* 5599 (1839), the trembling prisoners were led to a Kiev field where the Russian officers, judges, doctors and five hundred bludgeon-bearing soldiers were assembled. The younger brother asked to be first, hoping that when the soldiers saw the effects of their blows upon him, they would have more compassion for his older brother. After his third pass through the whipping line, he collapsed in a pool of his own blood. He was sent to a hospital to be revived in order to be transferred to Siberia.

The same punishment was then meted out to his brother. Under the hail of blows, his yarmulka fell to the earth and he bent down to pick it up, so that he shouldn't take a step bareheaded. The pounding didn't cease as he bent and the clubs smashed his nose and his lips. After his third traverse of the gantlet, he too fell unconscious to the ground, but the doctors were able to revive him.

Before they were transferred from the hospital to their exile, one of their *payos* and half of their beards were shaved with a razor and they deeply regretted being deprived of these mitzvos. When their father, Reb Moshe, heard of their misfortune, he died of a broken heart.

During this time, the Government began to suspect all Jewish presses of illicit printing and shut down all but two: one in Vilna and one in Kiev — where the censor could keep a constant watch on the works. Czar Nikolai also levied a heavy annual tax of 500 rubles on each of these presses. The censors were then instructed to review all previously printed books and to remove any objectionable lines or chapters.

಼

S UCH was the bitter outcome of a dispute that polarized European Jewry and of an insult to Rabbi Akiva Eiger, the *gaon* of the era. Reb Akiva was a man whose genius, nearly 150 years since his passing, still defies proper assessment. To untutored students, Reb Akiva Eiger's words are terse, a cryptic message of erudition; to those blessed with comprehension, his elucidating commentaries illuminate new vistas of learning.

No Jew was more despised by Posen Jewry than Mr. Ploni. He specialized in foreclosures and frequently expropriated properties and fortunes, adding them to his own vast estate. He used his influential position with the Prussian government to the disadvantage of the Jewish population.

His death brought celebration to the Jews of Posen, who hoped they could now recoup some of their stolen money. The chevra kadisha *refused to bury Ploni until they exacted an exorbitant sum from his family for the funeral. Not long after the burial, however, the* chevra kadisha *was summoned to appear in court on charges of extortion. The Rabbi and Rosh Yeshiva of Posen, Rabbi Akiva Ginns (Eiger) was also subpoenaed to the trial.*

Rabbi Akiva Eiger defended the action of the burial society by referring to a passage in the Talmud: 'All will rise at the time of the revival of the dead excluding those who lend with interest...' "This statement," Rabbi Eiger explained, "implies that no Jew is eternally interred into the earth. Actually one doesn't purchase a burial plot, but rents it, for at the time of the revival it will no longer be needed. However, for someone like Ploni who lent with interest, the sale of the plot is an irrevocable purchase. Is it any wonder that the price of a sale should significantly exceed that of a rental?"

The judge found it hard to disagree...

BORN IN 5522 (1762) to Rabbi Moshe Ginns (grandson of Rabbi Avraham Braudie) and his wife (the daughter of the first Rabbi Akiva Eiger — author of *Mishnas Rabbi Akiva Eiger*), Akiva was a child prodigy. At six years of age, by virtue of his amazing intellect, he had already outgrown the local *chinuch* opportunities in his native Eisenstadt, Hungary. Accordingly, young Akiva Ginns was sent to the renowned Mattersdorf Yeshiva, but even "Mattersdorf" could provide only temporary fulfillment for the young boy.

When Akiva was twelve, his father received a letter from his wife's brother, Rabbi Wolf Eiger, the *Rosh Yeshiva* of the illustrious Breslau Yeshiva in Germany. The letter contained a query which had confounded all the scholars at his yeshiva. Reb Moshe showed the question to his son, who had little trouble in finding an answer. Akiva's response, forwarded to his uncle, was received with more than enthusiasm: a coach was swiftly dispatched from Breslau to Mattersdorf to capture this prize for the yeshiva.

Entry into the Breslau yeshiva marked a turning point in Akiva's development. A mere teenager, he was awarded a *shiur*. (The honor of delivering a talmudic lecture was an indication of the yeshiva's recognition of his erudition.)

When Reb Wolf Eiger* had to travel out of town, he left the yeshiva in his young nephew's competent hands.

Word of Akiva's brilliance spread quickly and his eighteenth birthday was greeted by a delegation from Lissa, Poland. Object: matrimony. Reb Yitzhak Margolis, a wealthy Polish businessman, accompanied by two scholars entrusted with the job of verifying the prospective groom's reputation, wished to see and examine the famous prodigy in person. The meeting was attended by Akiva's uncle, the *Rosh Yeshiva*, and his father, who had travelled from Eisenstadt for the occasion.

To the vexation and chagrin of his family, Akiva remained silent throughout the testing. Dumbfounded by his performance, they interrupted the examination to convene a conference. "Akiva, what's the matter with you? Surely you know the answers to the questions posed!?"

Akiva explained that the tester had missed a *Tosefos* and misunderstood an interpretation of the Gemara. To answer the questions correctly would cause the examiner embarrassment, an eventuality far worse than losing the *shiduch*. They recommended that he solve his dilemma by abandoning the test and offering in its stead his own novel talmudic interpretation of an entirely different passage. The advice was followed to the glowing satisfaction of all present.

AKIVA's OVERWHELMING desire to spare someone embarrassment was a driving force in his life. Once, a Seder guest accidentally spilled wine on the Eigers' clean tablecloth. Rabbi Akiva Eiger nonchalantly slipped his hand

---

* Apparently Akiva Ginns, known to all as Akiva Eiger, had his last name switched in deference to his uncle, who taught him as a son. Thus, his name became identical to that of his maternal grandfather.

under the table and joggled the table leg, commenting immediately, "My, how shaky this table is..."

Rabbi Mordechai Benet once honored his guest, Rabbi Akiva Eiger, by inviting him to deliver a discourse to his Nickolsburg community. During the course of the lecture, Rabbi Benet raised so many challenging questions that he had practically taken over the podium. Afterwards, Rabbi Benet feared that he might have offended his venerable guest: He approached Reb Akiva and found the latter able to defend all of his points.

"Why didn't you answer thus when I challenged you?"

"My dear colleague," responded Reb Akiva, "you are the Rabbi of this town and I am merely passing through. Thank God I have my own congregation in Posen, but your honor here is of paramount importance..."

REB AKIVA was married in Lissa in 5540 (1780). There he spent the first years of his marriage engrossed in Torah study and enjoying his father-in-law's financial support. He then opened a yeshiva in Lissa which quickly became the focal point for students who flocked from afar to learn from a young master of unparalleled intellect. The function of his *shiurim* were to achieve ישרות השכל, a purification of thought — piercing analysis unencumbered by tangential concepts or even encyclopedic knowledge which might hinder clear thinking. His attitude toward Torah study is best described by his own words:

> " 'I rejoice at Your words like one who finds great booty...' (Psalms 119). One who is privileged to understand the words of Torah is comparable to one who finds a tremendous treasure, but can only transport a small fraction of it. His joy at the find is diminished by the realization that he must leave most of it behind.

> *"So is the Jew who learns Torah and uncovers new and novel interpretations... The more he learns the more he perceives how great and deep are the words of Torah — and how far he is from totally conquering it. 'I rejoice at Your words,' yet my joy is not complete, it is like one 'who finds a great booty,' for I realize that I cannot take it all with me..."*

THE MONETARY SUPPORT which Rabbi Akiva received from his father-in-law was cut off abruptly in 5550 (1790) when a fire destroyed most of Lissa. Rabbi Akiva's financial straits coupled with his father-in-law's insistence that he enter the rabbinate compelled him in 5552 to accept the position of Rabbi and communal leader in Markish Friedland, Germany.

Accepting this job entailed three things which were anathema to Reb Akiva: first, receiving remuneration for providing spiritual services (a distaste for which he had inherited from his father who worked as a laborer so as not to accept similar compensation); second, the responsibility of issuing halachic rulings; and third, the honor and prestige inherent in the position. His emotions were succinctly expressed in a letter to a friend in which he confided that he felt that the rabbinate was "a fate worse than death."

Four years later he wrote, "I would much prefer to be an attendant in a synagogue or a night-watchman than be a Rabbi. That way I could earn a living from the labor of my hands and learn most of the day..."

Despite his aversion to the job, he shouldered communal responsibility with selfless devotion:

> *In 5556 (1796) a deadly epidemic of cholera — the disease which was later to claim the Rabbi's own wife — broke out, plaguing nursing mothers in particular.*

Reb Akiva took to the podium and delivered a passionate plea for communal cooperation and assistance. He saw to it that orphans were placed in the homes of the wealthy and that healthy nursing mothers tended the deprived babies. Every foster mother had to undergo a weekly inspection by the Rabbi, who checked the baby's crib, layette and all other relevant sanitary conditions.

Reb Akiva also supervised the educational facilities in the town. Every Thursday afternoon, he tested all of the *cheder* children in the presence of their teachers.

With so hectic a schedule Reb Akiva had little time for leisure.

On one occasion, under the pretext of escorting him to a bris, Reb Akiva's sons led him on a long journey to a beautiful mansion in the hope that such a trip would provide rest and relaxation. When he arrived at the mansion Reb Akiva immediately started walking towards the end of the hall which was decorated with a huge wall mirror. Startled by his alacrity, his sons asked him where he was headed. "I saw such a distinguished looking Jew," he responded, "I felt that I must immediately go over and give 'Shalom aleichem'..."

Not one for gazing in mirrors, Reb Akiva had not recognized his own unfamiliar reflection. This was typical of a man of such an abstemious nature. During the week he never ate bread except where hospitality demanded that he do so in order for his guests to feel comfortable.

REB AKIVA'S first marriage came to a sad end after only sixteen years, when his beloved wife passed away. During her life she bore him four children, two of whom she was privileged to see wed shortly before her death.

No time was wasted in suggesting new matches to the bereaved Reb Akiva. His written response to one such offer recommended during the thirty-day mourning period, is regarded in yeshiva circles as a description of the ideal relationship between husband and wife:

> *"Can I forget my perfect love who bore and raised my children to worship and fear God? She stood at my side to allow me to study Torah, and nurtured my debilitated body and removed all monetary concerns from me...*
>
> *What man on earth knows her righteousness and modesty more than I? Often we discussed matters concerning fear of Heaven until midnight..."*

Reb Akiva eventually gave in to mounting pressure and accepted the very *shiduch* whose suggestion he had initially opposed. The bride was his former wife's sister's daughter, a factor which encouraged him to pursue the match and provide his father-in-law *nachas* by remaining, as it were, his son-in-law.

I N THE YEAR 5575 (1815) a delegation from Posen asked Reb Akiva to become the Rabbi of their town. Once again he faced the dilemma of getting more involved in a profession which he despised.

Posen was a larger city than Markish Friedland and would afford a greater opportunity to teach Torah and influence the masses. The Emancipation had wrought havoc on the Jewish youth of Markish Friedland, who fled to nearby metropolises. Even Markish Friedland's yeshiva was attended by out-of-town students who had come there only because Reb Akiva was its dean.

The position in Posen, whose greater Jewish population was in excess of 50,000, entailed far greater responsibilities and obligations. In addition, Reb Akiva devoted time to other communal pursuits. He visited Posen's infirm each week and cared for the needy and indigent.

> *A poor man once complained to Rabbi Akiva Eiger that he didn't have enough money to provide a dowry for his daughter. Reb Akiva instructed the family to make an initial investment of just five reichsthaller, and he would personally underwrite the rest of the cost...*

ALMOST ALL of Rabbi Akiva Eiger's writings come from his period as Rabbi in Markish Friedland.* From the time that Reb Akiva eventually accepted the Posen offer in 1816, his writing came to a virtual standstill and he refused to respond to out of town inquirers.

Although Posen possessed a vibrant Jewish community and an excellent yeshiva, it wasn't spared from the effects of the emerging Reform movement headquartered nearby. When the adherents of the Reform movement held a convention in Hamburg in 5579 (1819), Reb Akiva, aided by his son-in-law, the "Chasam Sofer"** took steps to counteract the Reform platforms. Four years later, Reform groups lobbied the government to discontinue *Talmud*

---

* In Markish Friedland Rabbi Akiva Eiger's day commenced at 4:00 A.M. His morning was devoted to private study, and lectures in Talmud and *Shulchan Aruch.* After lunch he relaxed while looking over the queries which he had received that day. Starting at 8 P.M. he began writing his responsa, which he completed by midnight.

** Reb Moshe Sofer married Reb Akiva's eldest daughter from his first marriage.

*Torah*s and to intervene in the curricula of yeshivos. Once again Reb Akiva joined forces with his son-in-law to combat these efforts that threatened yeshiva excellence and strict mitzva adherence.

> *During the course of his travels Rabbi Akiva came to Warsaw where the case of a meshumad who refused to issue his wife a get was brought to his attention. The* Beis Din *had long since ruled that the man must award his wife a divorce, but he persisted in ignoring the ruling.*
>
> *Rabbi Akiva instructed his attendants to bring this man to him. Reb Akiva greeted him by saying, "My friend, let us sit down and learn a* Mishna *together..." Reb Akiva opened up* Mishnayos Kiddushin *and began to read, " 'A woman is acquired in marriage in three ways and is released from marriage in two ways: She is acquired by money, deed, and relations... She is* released from marriage by divorce or her husband's death...'
>
> *"You see, it is very clear. You have one of two options..."*
>
> *The fellow ridiculed both the* Mishna *and the Rabbi and left hurriedly. Just a few steps outside the door he began to feel faint. He subsequently lost consciousness and within minutes, was dead.*

R ABBI AKIVA EIGER'S greatest devotion was to his students. Personal principles he held inviolable could be overlooked for his pupils' sakes. In his later years, for example, although he had stopped writing endorsements for books, when one student pleaded for an approbation he acquiesced, reasoning that if he couldn't refuse a son, he had no right to refuse a student.

Reb Akiva never referred to a pupil as a *talmid*, claiming, "who knows who has learned more from whom?" (Introduction to *Responsa*). He introduced his instructions with "maybe" or "perhaps" rather than "must" or "should." Reb Akiva's students felt that their *rebbe* wasn't *teaching* them the Talmud, but rather was *learning* it together with them.

He impressed upon them the criterion of a "legitimate question" and the difference between one question and another. A צ״ע is not the same as a צע״ג and this is yet different from די יראה עיני (Reb Shlomo Heiman). And as any yeshiva student knows, regardless of the classification that Rabbi Akiva Eiger assigned to the question, a "*Reb Akiva Eiger's a kasha*" is a most complex one. Deceptive in its apparent simplicity, its answer would elude one of lesser intellect than Reb Akiva (Reb Yaakov Kamenetsky).

RABBI AKIVA EIGER'S written legacy, words written hastily and without precision on Friday afternoons when students weren't around (*Drush VeChidush Kesubos* 10) leaves no room for conjecture concerning Rabbi Akiva Eiger's genius. *Gilyon HaShas* was initially written in the margin of his Talmud. His daily learning quota of eighty folios a day, tallying up to a monthly completion of *shas*, left him little time to sit down with a conventional quill and notebook. His commentary on *Mishna*, written ostensibly for the layman, remains a scholarly work of the highest order, as does his commentary on *Shulchan Aruch*.

Close to 800 of his responsa have been recovered, including *Drush VeChidush* and *Kovetz Shailos U'Teshuvos Reb Akiva Eiger*. Reb Akiva Eiger never wrote novellae on Talmud *per se*, assuming with typical humility that anything that he could think of had already been written (*Teshuvos* 212).

אי לאו האי ע״ש — *"If not for that* erev Shabbos..." — *five cryptic words mentioned in passing in the writings of Rabbi Akiva Eiger's son. They allude, according to authoritative tradition, to an unusual visit Reb Akiva received one auspicious Friday afternoon...*

Reb Akiva had decided, only one day earlier, that his writings were not the absolute truth. His written Torah thoughts, he had reasoned, were too pilpulistic and not close enough to the simple pshat. *Therefore he had resolved to burn all of his writings that Saturday night and not leave a trace of what he deemed to be false.*

On Friday, however, three strikingly distinguished gentlemen knocked on his door. Rabbi Akiva Eiger had never seen these men before.

"Shalom aleichem. *We are emissaries of the Celestial* Beis Din *and have come to inform you that you have no right to destroy the writings. Having written them down, you relinquished ownership of your thoughts and they are now the property of the Jewish people. It is unworthy of a man such as yourself to steal from others..." And they vanished.*

Reb Akiva had no choice but to obey. He had not disclosed his plans to anyone, so that there was only one possible way for these "gentlemen" to have known his intentions. And who would dare defy the orders of angels?

L ATER IN LIFE Reb Akiva was afflicted with a debilitating disease. According to his own testimony, from the age of fifteen he had always suffered from illness. Yet infirmity never interfered with his long and demanding learning schedule.

By the time Reb Akiva was 76, he could no longer talk. Just before he lost his power of speech he confided to a doctor what he believed to be the source of his problem. "From the time I was a little boy I never chewed my food so as not to derive any pleasure therefrom. I merely cut it up and swallowed it as is..." Notwithstanding his loss of the ability to converse, and to the astonishment of all, he was still able to say *Amen;* the first verse of *Shema;* the blessing over *tefillin; Yehai shmei rabba;* and "My mouth speaks the praise of the Lord," the introductory phrase to *Shemoneh Esrei*, which he repeated often.

In Ellul 5597 (1837) disease overcame a body that struggled to continue learning and disseminating Torah. He left instructions forbidding eulogies and for his tombstone to read simply: "Here lies the Rabbi, Reb Akiva Eiger who was a servant to those who served God in Markish Friedland and here in Posen."

His will regarding eulogies was reluctantly fulfilled; however, the rabbis of Posen took the liberty of changing the wording of the tombstone from "Reb" Akiva Eiger to *"Rabbeinu"* — our teacher... They dared alter no other of the words of the master who had referred to himself as a student and servant.

Reb Berel and
the Reign of Emmes

EB YOSEF DOV (Berel) Soloveitchik, the renowned dean of the Brisker Yeshiva in Jerusalem, was the scion of one of the most famous rabbinic families in Eastern Europe. What he accomplished in his brief life time was nothing less than a revolution in the contemporary concept of yeshiva study. To appreciate his contribution, however, one must first appreciate his past.

In a town called Brisk, where talmudic erudition reigned supreme and intensive learning was the ultimate value, one man rose above all others. His name was Chaim, son of Yosef Dov Halevi, Soloveitchik, better known as "Reb Chaim Brisker." Born in 5613 (1853) he became the outstanding Torah figure of his time, and generated a departure in yeshiva curriculum and methodology.

Reb Chaim's famous learning technique which has become the bedrock of higher yeshiva erudition, was his ability to itemize: שני דינים — two principles, two rules, two categories — the object and the person, the active and the passive, the general and the specific, etc. Is the "fulfillment of the commandment to destroy *chometz*" before Passover a law regarding a *Jew* who must remove *chometz* from his possession, or that the *object* of *chometz* must be destroyed during this period? By breaking everything down into specific categories, most questions and problems became either irrelevant or inapplicable.

Reb Chaim, like all of his descendants, was a true zealot — zealous about causes and zealous about his love for his fellow Jew.

> *"I am alone with nothing to eat,"* whimpered a woman in an advanced stage of pregnancy at the threshold of the Soloveitchik home. Reb Chaim asked his wife why the women of the town were not helping — but the Rebbitzen did not respond and pretended not to have heard the question.

> Reb Chaim continued to probe until the Rebbitzen disclosed that this woman's husband had abandoned her over eleven months ago... "How much more so," interjected Reb Chaim, "is she all alone and dependent upon our help. Hurry and prepare a room for her where she will be our guest for the next few weeks, and then we will provide a monthly stipend for her and the child for the coming two years..."

> Two weeks later a bris was held in the very same house which had lodged the mother — the guest of Reb Chaim Brisker...*[1]

---

* This story highlights Reb Chaim's magnanimity towards his fellow man; it does not, of course, imply that Reb Chaim condoned the woman's behavior.

YITZHAK ZE'EV — Velvel, was Reb Chaim's youngest son. In 5652 (1892) when Velvel was four years old, the Volozhiner Yeshiva (where his father, grandfather and great-grandfather had been *Roshei Yeshiva*) closed down and his family moved to Brisk. It is reasonable to assume that Velvel received a staunch resistance to the "Enlightenment movement" — which precipitated the Volozhiner Yeshiva's closing. From Brisk he inherited opposition to secular values in general, and he took the initiative to counteract them.

Steeped in Torah learning and zealous in his observance of mitzvos, Reb Velvel (the Brisker Rav) was a beacon of confidence. He didn't flinch at any intimidation from the outside world nor succumb to pressures from within.

Many students, along with several notables, appealed to the Brisker Rav to permit electioneering prior to the Motzai Shabbos Kehilla *(an organization responsible to the government) ballot. "If the Rav won't allow us to broadcast our platform, the irreligious camp will win by a landslide," they argued, and the Brisker Rav grudgingly agreed.*

Ironically, the irreligious and the religious hired the same printer to run off their placards and literature. Apparently, for an additional fee, the printer showed the irreligious campaign organizers the text of the adherents of the Brisker Rav. The irreligious then printed an even more profanatory placard, strongly condemning and debasing the Brisker Rav. All of this resulted in a delay in producing the placards for the religious camp and they weren't ready until erev Shabbos.

Because of the late hour, the students grabbed the posters directly off the printing press and ran to show them to the Brisker Rav for his approval before posting them throughout the city. Reb Velvel, however, took the placards and locked them in his room. "It is erev Shabbos and winning every seat in the election isn't worth a risk of desecrating the Sabbath..." "But Rebbe, if we don't paste up our placards, the residents of Brisk will only see the posters of the irreligious and will be lured by their propaganda. We'll be careful to stop affixing the posters well before Shabbos. Please. PLEASE!!"

"Just as there is a mitzva to fight the 'Enlightenists,' likewise is there a mitzva to observe the Shabbos, and I cannot permit any risks in that regard!"

That Shabbos, Brisk was saturated with placards denouncing the religious platform and attacking the Brisker Rav — and no pro-religious posters appeared at all.

Nevertheless, it was beyond the imagination of the residents of Brisk, who had all of Shabbos to study the propaganda, what the Brisker Rav could have done to deserve such insults and ridicule. He had not posted any derisive remarks about the town's irreligious residents or their leaders. In fact, the "Enlightenist" posters appeared so unprovoked and in such poor taste that the religious camp emerged the overwhelming victors in the election — out of all proportion to their numbers.[2]

❀

THE SOLOVEITCHIK DYNASTY founded in Volozhin, continued in Brisk and transported to Jerusalem with Reb Velvel's immigration in 5701 (1941), hasn't lost its momentum. Three of the Brisker Rav's sons (Yosef Dov, Dovid and Meir) are the founders of three yeshivos named and patterned after the Brisker legacy. There is no one acquainted with the yeshiva world who hasn't heard of "the Brisker Yeshivos," but it wasn't always that way...

When the Brisker Rav first came to *Eretz Yisrael,* a small group of *talmidim* clustered around him. These *talmidim* heard a daily *shiur* from the Rav. In 5710 (1950) the Brisker Rav instructed his eldest son, Yosef Dov (Reb Berel) to begin delivering a *shiur.* And so, at the age of 35, nine years before the death of his father, Reb Berel became a link in the chain.

In order to encourage *talmidim* to join Reb Berel's *shiur,* the Brisker Rav spoke to his son's students periodically. Reb Berel delivered his *shiur* in the Achva Shul, situated on Reishis Chachma Street in the Geula section of Jerusalem. This shul later housed the Brisker Yeshiva.

Within the walls of this simple shul, housing bare benches and rickety *shtenders,* "Brisk" was transformed from a geographic location and elitist-didactic term into a flourishing yeshiva open to anyone who qualified. Starting with just a handful of students learning *maseches Makkos,* the Yeshiva grew to over 200 married and single *talmidim.*

THE BURGEONING OF "BRISK" defies all norms of yeshiva expansion. It doesn't have *rebbeim,* a *mashgiach,* an executive director, fund solicitors, a dormitory, dining facilities, a secretary, a telephone, stationery, a mailbox, or even a yeshiva building. In fact, Reb Berel used to remove the foil lining from cigarette boxes and write all the daily information pertinent to the yeshiva on the back of that little paper. "This is the office," Reb Berel would say, tapping the silver scrap stuffed in his breast pocket...[3]

How could such a "yeshiva" — as inappropriate as such a term sounds in light of the above — exist, let alone thrive? The answer lies in its *Rosh Yeshiva*, his *shiur* and his mission. Reb Berel viewed himself as the authentic transmitter of the Soloveitchik-Brisker Torah. He could have spread his own wings, developed and related his own Torah thoughts — as he was so eminently capable of doing. Revealing his own genius would certainly have won him fame in the Torah world as a prominent, original *gaon* and *rosh yeshiva*. But Reb Berel chose otherwise.

While Reb Chaim's *talmidim* became the next generation's *gedolim* and *roshei yeshiva,* the Brisker Yeshiva in Jerusalem became the conduit of the Brisker legacy. Reb Chaim and the Brisker Rav would continue to deliver their *shiurim* — through their progeny. Reb Berel was a relay station: the voice was his but the ideas, concepts and methodology were those of his father and grandfather.

To assist in the perfection of the transmission, the Yeshiva's syllabus was limited to *seder Kodshim* (and *maseches Nazir*), one of the most cryptic and esoteric sections of the Talmud. *Kodshim* deals primarily with sacrifices and Temple rites. The Chofetz Chaim advocated learning *Kodshim* so that Jews will be familiar and prepared for the advent of the Messiah.

It isn't clear why the Brisker Rav specifically promoted *Kodshim* as a method by which to develop the "Brisker *derech*." Some have suggested that the other sections of the Talmud are too thoroughly treated by the earlier and later commentaries to allow for rigorous, original and independent expression. *Kodshim*, on the other hand, is only nominally discussed.[4] Others contend that Reb Velvel's greatest proficiency was achieved in *Kodshim*, perhaps because it was this section that he studied the most under the aegis of his father.[5]

By concentrating on *Kodshim*, the Brisker Rav, via Reb Berel, highlighted its salience. The critico-conceptual method of minutely dividing and explaining every passage and opinion was applied to tractates *Zevachim, Menachos, Temurah, Bechoros* and *Nazir*. In short, Reb Chaim developed the Brisker *derech*, the Brisker Rav applied it, and Reb Beryl disseminated it by opening a yeshiva for its study.

THERE WAS one other principle which Reb Beryl administered as unyieldingly in the Yeshiva as his forebears had in Brisk — *Emmes*.* An indolent, superficial thinker was alien to the Yeshiva. *Emmes* with its exacting demands and strict specifications reigned unchallenged — without compromise or vacillation. A thought or essay which did not fit into the austere parameters of *Emmes* was invalid and rejected out of hand. Since *Emmes* is unrelenting, so must Torah study be. *Aggadata*, interpretations of Scriptural verses, *piyuttim*, etc. must all be placed under the microscope of *Emmes* and not be relegated to hermeneutics or the like. This didn't make study in the Yeshiva easy — but it did make it prestigious.

---

* The Brisker concept of *Emmes* is synonymous with "purity" and is not defined as "honesty" or "truth."

Brisk also demanded conformity in political outlook and personal activity, for *Emmes* cannot tolerate a partial truth, "good intentions" or an "end justifying the means." Reb Berel became the watchdog of *Emmes* in *Eretz Yisrael* and the expression "What will they say in Brisk?" has become a moral barometer.

When yeshivos and *chadorim* wished to accept Israeli government assistance and subsidies, Reb Berel intervened. If you accept their money you may fall prey to their supervision, he reasoned. A yeshiva cannot allow itself to be subject to outside influences. For this very reason his grandfather, great-grandfather and great-great-grandfather closed the doors of Volozhin.

Likewise, when the Likud came to power in 1977 and offered numerous incentives for the Agudath Israel party to join their coalition government, Reb Berel objected vehemently. Joining forces with non-religious factors was unthinkable to one schooled in the teachings of Brisk. While the Aguda party celebrated its achievements and basked in the concessions granted by the Begin government, Reb Berel looked on in disdain.

REB BERYL did not have to rely only on his lineage for the right to police *Emmes*, for he embodied the notion in pedagogy and lifestyle. His house was furnished as sparingly as the Yeshiva. It was a crowded, two-bedroom apartment with cracked, peeling walls, a crumbling floor, and a couch which consisted of protruding springs and steel bars partially covered by worn fabric. Into this cramped apartment 100 *talmidim* crowded to hear their master's *shiur*. (Four morning and three afternoon *shiurim* were delivered weekly to different groups; a *shiur* in *Zeraim* was given at night to a select group of veteran students; plus a *shiur* in *Parsha,* delivered every *Motzai Shabbos.*) The waiting list to get into "*shiur*" was usually eleven months long and was regulated by the number of people who could fit into the house.

Reb Berel saw to it that unparalleled standards of truth and honesty governed the Yeshiva. He would not accept a donation to the Yeshiva unless he could verify the purity of its source. Indeed, the slightest doubt would disqualify a contribution.

For example, he would refuse a donation from a woman unless he knew for certain that her husband consented. Anonymous donations were not accepted, and it goes without saying that money obtained illegally or from a non-observer was refused.* He had an assurance from his father that a yeshiva will succeed only if it ran on "*kosher gelt.*"

When it came to distributing money, his standards were just as high. Every *Rosh Chodesh* (and never a day later), Reb Berel disbursed a modest stipend to *bochurim* (who had to tend to their own needs in the absence of yeshiva facilities) and married students. What he gave was exact.

Reb Berel had an elaborate system for calculating a person's needs. He would question a student to determine whether he received any outside assistance or if his wife was working. Did he have a refrigerator, a washing machine, etc.? In the Brisker Yeshiva, money was disbursed according to need — not scholastic ability or *yichus.*

---

* A recommendation from one's *rosh yeshiva* was mandatory in order to be eligible for a fellowship from the Keren Gavrilovitz fund in Tel Aviv. Once, when a Brisker student applied for the scholarship, Reb Berel investigated the source and background of the fund for over two weeks, before agreeing to write an endorsement.

One who wanted to witness the true meaning of הנותן בעין
יפה ובסבר פנים יפות — giving generously and with a pleasant
countenance — had to see Reb Berel distribute the money.
He maintained that the person accepting the money was
doing *him* the favor. "I am merely a גבאי צדקה — 'charity
custodian' " — he would say to reassure anyone hesitant
about receiving money from a man who barely had enough
to live. Whatever money may have accumulated, he gave
away and never put any aside for the coming month — his
trust in God was absolute.

In honor of *Yom Tov*, he doubled the students' stipend
and it was only the second portion which was occasionally
late in coming. (The second portion was designated for the
holiday still weeks away, otherwise it too would have been
available on the first of the month — no matter what
hardship that would have entailed.)

Reb Berel also arranged the support of dozens of
families who never knew how their income arrived. He also
paid the water, electricity and heating bills of the Achva Shul
which hosted the Yeshiva.

REB BEREL was equally concerned with the spiritual
and the physical needs of his students. He was a
mentor *par excellence*, and would speak at length with his
talmidim about any matter. His wisdom and perception in
so many disciplines resulted in his students' seeking his
counsel in every area:

> *One day in the middle of a* shiur *a* talmid *came
> panting into the house. Reb Berel, it was known,
> would do anything not to miss or interrupt a* shiur. *But
> when he saw his student's frenetic state, he stood up
> and asked what the problem was.*
>
> *"My wife is in labor, and the doctor wants to*

perform a Caesarean section — I don't know if I should agree..."

Reb Berel closed his Gemara and ran arm-in-arm with his student to the hospital. Not only did he want to verify the facts for himself, but he didn't trust his student to think coherently or to instruct precisely in his condition.

The doctor, who had mocked the idea of consulting with a rabbinic authority, changed his mind after meeting and discussing the matter with Reb Berel...[6]

Such was the devotion Reb Berel had for his *talmidim.* He would provide them with everything — except halachic decisions. In this regard, he, like his father and many other Briskers, was an expert in avoiding *shailos* (halachic rulings). Rendering a halachic decision requires ruling in accordance with one opinion, to the exclusion of another. This is anathema to Briskers, who strive to reconcile every halachic opinion — even contradictory ones.

A S DEMANDING as Reb Berel was of his students in the realm of learning and *Emmes,* so was he when it came to *chessed:*

Reb Shmuel Dovid Movshovitz recommended to a friend of his from Petach Tikva that he attend the Brisker Yeshiva, and escorted him to the Rosh Yeshiva's *interview. Not long after the interview began, the new student emerged alabaster-white. "Shmuel Dovid, it didn't go well and I made a fool of myself." Movshovitz pressed him for details, but he despondently left for home without revealing what had happened.*

A few minutes later Reb Berel entered the beis midrash — *a rare occurrence* — *looking for Movshovitz. "Your friend started relating his* shtikel Torah *thought] and in the middle* — *I suppose out of nervousness* — *he became tongue-tied like a mute and he couldn't finish speaking."*

Three weeks later, during the Yeshiva recess, Movshovitz heard that Reb Berel was anxiously looking for him. He hurried to his Rebbe, who instructed him to fetch his friend right away so that Reb Berel could inform him personally that he had been accepted to the Yeshiva. "But he lives in Petach Tikva," protested Movshovitz.

"It doesn't matter. I discussed it with my father [who had passed away in the interim] and he ordered me to accept him immediately, or the bochur *may remain desolate for years over the incident." Movshovitz did as he was told and rushed to Petach Tikva to notify his friend.*

Reb Berel did far more than he was told. He accepted the bochur *into the Yeshiva and into his heart. Reb Berel noticed that this fellow's speech impediment had generated social problems and low self-esteem. His affection and care for this* bochur *was so great it seemed as if he considered himself responsible for the problem – all because of their initial encounter. Indeed Reb Berel personally undertook to "marry off" this student – and fulfilled his pledge...*[7]

It was very evident to Reb Berel that despite the Yeshiva's success in such minimal conditions, a permanent yeshiva building would eventually have to be sought. Indeed the Brisker Rav was the first one to finance this project by handing his son a few Pounds* earmarked for a building. Friends and supporters of the Yeshiva bought the home of the Brisker Rav and began to expand and add floors for this very purpose — but Reb Berel never lived to see the completion of this project.

HE DID LIVE to see his family's tradition carried on. He became a link in the Brisker chain that was forged with such scholarship and piety, that when it was severed Friday morning, the second of Adar Aleph 5741, the news spread pain and grief across the Torah globe. Tens of thousands of admirers and friends gathered outside that famous house on Menachem Street in Jerusalem where countless *shiurim* had been delivered in the Brisker tradition.

At the conclusion of the funeral service, Eliyahu Chaim Shapiro,[8] in the name of the students of the Brisker Yeshiva, announced that a new link had been added: Reb Berel's eldest son, Reb Avraham Yehoshua, who had already started giving *shiurim* in his father's lifetime, had been appointed the successor and *Rosh Yeshiva* of his father's Brisker Yeshiva.

* The "Pound" was the Israeli currency which preceded the Shekel.

Notes

1. *Ishim Veshitos*, Rabbi S.Y. Zevin, p. 77.
2. Rabbi Y. Galinsky.
3. His students.
4. *Ibid.*
5. His family.
6. His students.
7. *Ibid.*
8. *Hamodia*, 4 Adar I, 5741.

Reb Leib Gurwicz:
The Lion's Share

Leadership is one ship which cannot pull into a safe port in a storm. Rabbi Leib ("lion" in Yiddish) Gurwicz assumed the lion's share in leading British Jewry, as dean of its foremost yeshiva. The roar that issued forth from the Gateshead *Rosh Yeshiva* heralded, in the words of the Chofetz Chaim, redemption for the Torah community of England and salvation for the local level of learning. In actuality, the confluence of circumstances which led to his immigration to England represented a "redemption and salvation" for himself as well.

✥Rue Britannia

LIKE MANY *roshei yeshiva*, Eliyahu Lopian bore the financial as well as the spiritual yoke of his yeshiva. Responsibility for the material support of the institution resulted in frequent trans-European trips. On one such fundraising mission, Reb Elya had traversed a great deal of Europe and was in Germany on the last leg of his journey. Just before departing, he asked a local Jew for directions. The latter responded, "*Rebbe*, come with me and I will show you the way." When they came to a dark alley, a gun was placed at Reb Elya's head and the proverbial option offered.

His money gone, Reb Elya was now in a bind. He could not return to the same villages he had solicited just one month earlier, but he also could not return home empty-handed. The one and only alternative lay across the sea in England.

England at that time, from the perspective of an observant Jew, was a world apart. It's only connection to Europe was its geographic proximity. As far as a Lithuanian *rosh yeshiva* was concerned, it might just as well have been thousands of miles away. British Jewry was by and large irreligious and thoroughly ignorant of Torah learning and mitzvos.

REB ELYA decided to employ the *Goral HaGra** to determine if he should embark on the trip. The *goral* landed on the verse: "I will go down with you to Egypt and I will surely bring you up again..." (*Bereishis* 46:4), an apparently clear indication that he should proceed with the journey.

When Reb Elya arrived in England he encountered a friend of his from Kelm, Rabbi Aharon Bakst — the *Rosh Yeshiva* and founder of the Etz Chaim Yeshiva in London. "Reb Elya," began Rabbi Bakst, "I must travel to Europe for a short visit. Perhaps you would be so kind as to fill in for me in my absence?"

Rabbi Bakst never returned to England. Reb Elya was left with a yeshiva to direct, another yeshiva to fund and a wife and thirteen children back in Kelm. What was he to do? He realized that the yeshiva in Kelm could survive without him, for he was not its sole *rosh yeshiva*. Furthermore,

---

* The *Goral HaGra*, literally, "lottery of the Vilna Gaon," is a method of determining action in accord with the implications of a biblical verse drawn at random.

there was no dearth of *roshei yeshiva* in interbellum Lithuania.

And so in 5688 (1928) Reb Elya sent for his family to pack their belongings and join him in England. After arriving at a difficult decision, its execution became even harder...

Reb Elya's father-in-law, Rabbi Yitzhak Dovid Rotman, a renowned *tzadik* who lived in Jerusalem, heard from an Englishman what the norms of religious observance in England were at that time.

"I thought I took a God-fearing son-in-law!" he wrote in fury to Reb Elya. "How could you abandon Lithuania for such a wilderness?!" To his daughter he wrote even stronger words: "If your husband does not agree to return from London to Kelm you must insist on a divorce!"

But she didn't heed her father's counsel. The Lopians managed to raise their thirteen children with the highest Torah standards despite their presence on British soil. Local *shiduch* opportunities, however, presented a problem.

I N 5694 (1934) Reb Elya and his eldest daughter, Leiba, returned to Europe in search of a suitable match. Already long-removed from the Lithuanian scene, Reb Elya turned for suggestions to his close friend from his days in the Kelmer *Beis HaMussar,* Reb Yeruchom Levovitz, the *Mashgiach* of the Mirrer Yeshiva.

There were many older unmarried students at the Mirrer Yeshiva because of the shortage of appropriate matches;* however, Reb Yeruchom rejected them all but one particular young man who had already left the Yeshiva. He had been one of the *Mashgiach*'s favorites and his qualifications met Reb Elya's criteria: the man who would

---

* The Bais Yaakov girls' school system was still in its infancy.

marry Leiba had to not only excel in learning but possess innately — rather than acquired — superior character traits.

"Go to the Brisker Rav," Reb Yeruchom advised, "and ask for 'Leibeleh Malater.' He is the *illui* you are looking for. You will find in this young man more humility, acuity in learning, and fear of Heaven than in any other."

Reb Yeruchom was correct. Reb Aryeh Ze'ev (Leib) Gurwicz was just that.

❧The Young Lion

AT THE AGE of thirteen, Leib bade a final farewell to his family in Malat, Poland before starting off for *yeshiva ketana* in Lithuania. His father, Reb Moshe Aharon Kushelevsky, descendant of a long line of *melamdim*, was the Rabbi of this small town where few of the residents were observant. His mother was a direct descendant of the Vilna Gaon, a fact which accounted for Leib's adoption of the customs and stringencies of the *Gaon*.

Leib's willingness to leave home at bar mitzva age was typical of the self-sacrificing attitude towards learning that remained with him the rest of his life. It was no small matter for a boy so young to abandon his family knowing that he would probably never see them again. His family's impoverished circumstances and the existing means of transportation precluded any possibility of returning.*

* Twelve years later Leib met his brother on Tisha B'Av in Ligmiyan. This town was in Poland but its Jewish cemetery was in Lithuanian territory. Somehow the Jews managed to convince the authorities of those two contentious countries that they must visit the graveyard on Tisha B'Av. And so for hundreds of Jews separated by a tense border, the Ninth of Av became an annual holiday for family reunions and the exchange of messages.

On a cold winter morning, Leib boarded the horse and cart which would take him to the Lithuanian frontier. Once there, he would have to slip across undetected and hope that the border police weren't shooting on that day. Before saying goodbye, his father took off his only coat and handed it to his son. "How can I take your coat when I know that you will suffer in the cold?" Leib protested. "I have already learned in yeshiva," responded his father, "and am no longer on the threshold of an advancement in Torah growth as you are. Therefore, you are the one who deserves a coat..."

Leib was so inspired by his father's gesture and parting words that from the day he arrived at the famed Vilkomirer Yeshiva in Lithuania he was always the first one into the *beis midrash* and the last one to leave...

THE TIME spent in the Vilkomirer Yeshiva, headed by Reb Elyah Kramerman and Reb Leib Rubin, was pivotal in Leibeleh Malater's development. He quickly established himself as the yeshiva's most diligent student and one of its sharpest minds.

After a year and a half in Vilkomirer, Leib journeyed to Vilna in the hope of visiting his family, which had resettled there. (As part of the Treaty of Versailles, Vilna had once again become Lithuanian.) Coincidental with Leib's visit was the arrival of the Mirrer Yeshiva which, along with several other yeshivos such as Slabodka and Radin, had fled deep into Russia during World War I. Vilna was only a temporary stopover for the Yeshiva which was waiting for the situation to stabilize so that it could return to Mir.

Leib never got to see his father, who had been called back to Malat, a town which subsequently reverted to

Polish control. He did, however, become one of the youngest students to join the Mirrer Yeshiva as a result of his visit.

AFTER A FEW YEARS in the Mir, Leib had to have his Polish passport altered. Lithuania (where he was learning) had a hostile relationship with its Polish neighbor, and Polish nationals were liable for expulsion.*

The nearest passport office was in Baranovitch, where Reb Elchonon Wasserman's yeshiva was located. There was a student in the Baranovitch Yeshiva who had the necessary connections to forge a passport; however, the procedure required that Leib adopt a new name. He chose his mother's maiden name — Gurwicz — as his surname and thus was he known for the rest of his life.

While in Baranovitch, Leib decided to visit Reb Elchonon's yeshiva and entered in the middle of the *Rosh Yeshiva*'s *shiur*. During the course of the *shiur* Leib posed a question which so impressed the famous *Rosh Yeshiva* that he pleaded with Leib to remain and learn with him.

Leib obliged, but in actuality, he had no choice. Unable to pay the fee the *bochur* demanded for arranging his new passport, he committed himself to learning קצות החושן with the *bochur* for a year, in lieu of payment.

After Leib had learned in the "Mir" for eight years, the

---

* Actually, Leib would have preferred to travel to *Eretz Yisrael* to learn but he had sought the blessing of Rabbi Yisrael Yaakov Lubchanski for the venture. The Rabbi's words could only have been construed as a blessing if Leib were to remain where he was... With *Eretz Yisrael* no longer an option, he had to quickly rectify his status as an illegal alien.

Rosh Yeshiva, Reb Eliezer Yehuda Finkel and the *Mashgiach,* Reb Yeruchom Levovitz, to whom Leib had become very attached, recommended that he travel to study under the Brisker Rav. Once again Leib was one of the youngest among a group of towering scholars such as Rabbis Leib Mallin, Mordechai Ginsburg and Michel Feinstein. The Brisker Rav took an exceptional liking to Leib and even awarded him his greatest accolade: ר' לייב קען לערנען — "Reb Leib knows how to learn." Yeshiva students are well aware of how great a learning ability is implied by the Brisker Rav's compliment of "knowing how to learn..."

⚘The Match is Made

I T WAS AFTER Leib had been studying under the Brisker Rav for two years that Reb Eliyahu Lopian arrived in search of the *bochur* Reb Yeruchom had so highly recommended for Reb Elya's daughter. Reb Elya's visit resulted in Leib's enjoying the unusual privilege of having not only the Mirrer Yeshiva come to him, but his bride as well.

After meeting and observing the prospective groom, Reb Elya was convinced that everything that he had heard was true, and the *"shiduch"* was consummated. It was understood that the couple would wed and remain in Poland.

During the course of the engagement, however Leibs prospective mother-in-law died at the age of 49. Leiba wrote from England to her *chossan* that her mother's untimely death ruled out travelling to Poland. Even after their marriage she would be obliged to remain in England to take care of her younger siblings. The message was clear.

REB YERUCHOM, the *shadchan*, was unable to decide whether to allow Reb Leib to journey to England. He advised him to seek the aging Chofetz Chaim's counsel and blessing, and Leib complied.

Instead of a direct response, however, the Chofetz Chaim repeated the following verses three times:

> *"Blessed be He who spoke, and the world came into being; blessed be He who created the universe. Blessed be He who says and performs. Blessed be He who decrees and fulfills. Blessed be He who has mercy on the world. Blessed be He who has mercy on all creatures. Blessed be He who grants a fair reward to those who revere Him. Blessed be He who lives forever and exists eternally. Blessed be He who redeems and saves..."*

Those who were present thought that the Chofetz Chaim was repeating himself out of forgetfulness. But Leib understood that going to England would be in the category of *"Blessed be he who redeems and saves."*

AFTER A DATE was set for Leib's wedding, his *kalla* wrote with astonishment: "How can we get married in your father's absence? I insist that your father join us for the *simcha* and I suggest that all the presents and money we receive for our wedding go to paying his fare."

Leiba prevailed and a ticket was sent to Reb Moshe Aharon Kushelevsky. From the time that he arrived in England until the day he left he seemed always to be crying. The last time he had seen his son was when Leib was a thirteen-year-old boy and now he was a distinguished *talmid chacham*, getting married in England! Indeed, the only extant picture of Leib's wedding depicts the *chossan* and *kalla* and a hand tightly clutching a well-used handkerchief. The hand belonged to Reb Moshe Aharon — a man overcome with emotion.

A few years after Reb Kushelevsky returned to Europe, he met a violent death at the hands of the Nazis. The turn of events which had brought Reb Elya, and subsequently Leib to England, spared them from the entire Nazi horror.

F ROM THE DAY of his marriage Leib lived in his father-in-law's home, which housed twelve children. The children loved their new brother-in-law — especially his easygoing nature. They found it difficult to relate to their father, who was totally absorbed in spiritual pursuits, and enjoyed their new surrogate parent who served the triple role of father, brother-in-law and friend all in one. Leib and Leiba's presence in the house was as necessary for the family as for themselves — their financial situation ruled out any other alternative.

Reb Leib Gurwicz delivered a *shiur* in his father-in-law's Etz Chaim Yeshiva, and also served as Rabbi of the Great Garden Synagogue in the East End of London. In that era, *chillul Shabbos* was the norm for London's Jews. For this reason Reb Leib didn't allow his children out of the house on Shabbos lest they witness the desecration which transpired in a Jewish neighborhood.

Reb Leib once related that when he came to England he noticed that the paper in which fish was wrapped was covered with handwritten Torah novellae. The proprietor of the fish store used his father's chidushim *as a means of packaging the fish, as he knew of no other function for the paper...*

❀ The Tin-Hut Yeshiva

A S WORLD WAR II escalated, a considerable influx of Jewish refugees began to pour onto the English coast. At that time there were two routes from Europe to England: either by a trans-Europe train and then by boat across the English channel, or by plying the North Sea and docking in northern England.

The second route existed long before the mass exodus precipitated by World War II. Sea traffic from the north resulted in the establishment of a northern port on the River Tyne, which flows from the North Sea. This port, straddling the twin cities of Newcastle and Gateshead, is separated by the river. At the turn of the century, it burgeoned into a major inland port to accommodate the increase in sea traffic.

Many Jews fleeing Europe followed this sea lane and settled in the larger of the two cities, Newcastle, where opportunities and amenities for Jews were scarce.

A small group of these Jewish settlers realized that the only way to continue in the path of their fathers and avoid the temptation of assimilation, was to break away from the Newcastle community. Accordingly, in the early 1920s, a cluster of religious Jews crossed the river and settled in Gateshead. They quickly erected a tin hut to serve as their shul not far from the river which had brought them to the British Isles.

With the semblance of a community already established around that rickety structure, they sought a *shochet* who would meet their scrupulous standards. A letter was dispatched to the Chofetz Chaim asking him to recommend a candidate. The nominee was Reb Dovid Dryan, a man who could have been employed as a *tzadik* if not for the fact that he earned his living from preparing meat.

REB DOVID viewed his slaughtering as a side line; he was chiefly engaged in fulfilling a mission. "A Jewish community must have a yeshiva," he maintained — an idea which sounded preposterous to the local residents. "Where will you get students and funding?" they questioned scornfully. But Reb Dovid was undaunted. Oblivious to their ridicule, he set out to recruit students.

> *After he succeeded in persuading one boy and his parents to join his enterprise, he felt he could begin. The yeshiva was housed in the community's tin hut shul, which was more than adequate for the initial student body. On the opening day of the "yeshiva" Reb Dovid entered Gateshead's solitary store which carried kosher items, and said, "Please put this bread and butter on the 'yeshiva's account...' "*

This first recruit served as a nucleus for the earliest students of "Yeshivas Bais Yosef," Gateshead. A yeshiva must have a *rosh yeshiva* and so Reb Dovid turned to the Chofetz Chaim to select the appropriate scholar. Rabbi Nachman Landynsky, a graduate of the Novardoker Yeshiva was the sage's choice. Only one schooled in the "outreach doctrine" of Novardok would be willing to subject himself to such an exile.

Under the leadership of Rabbi Landynsky, the Yeshiva began to grow until its enrollment numbered thirty students. In the late 1930s, however, a trickle of European emigrants began to escape to northern England, among them several *bochurim* who wished to continue their studies. Consequently, the Yeshiva began to expand and Rabbi Landynsky felt that it now needed a *mashgiach*. He offered the job to his co-Novardoker, Reb Eleazer Kahan — who accepted.

THE MATERIAL responsibilities of the Yeshiva remained in the hands of Reb Dovid Dryan. He found that the tangible existence of the Yeshiva didn't make fundraising any easier. Wherever he went, people refused to accept the new reality and greeted him with ridicule. But the Yeshiva's poverty was no laughing matter.

Another factor which impeded the Yeshiva's development was the local climate and population. The weather in Gateshead is almost perpetually cold and rainy and the air is laden with soot from extensive coal mining in the region. The clouds, like the *shtenders* of the Yeshiva, are carbon-coated and the odor of coal dust permeates the town.

The residents of the town were uneducated, ignorant coal miners who lived in drab, dismal surroundings. The town's major asset, from the perspective of the Yeshiva, was that its total absence of distractions made it conducive to learning.

With the conclusion of World War II, Gateshead — originally a haven for a select few — became a refuge for hundreds of devout Jews. The Yeshiva grew to a student body of 120 in a matter of weeks. But Reb Dovid still wasn't satisfied. A yeshiva of this size, he contended, must have a *kollel*. And a *kollel* must have a *rosh kollel*.

Rabbi Eliahu Dessler, a scholar whose profundity of thought and oratorical abilities had made a tremendous impact in London, was selected for the job. Several young men, including two of Reb Leib's brothers-in-law, Chaim Shmuel and Laib Lopian, moved from London to Gateshead to join the new *kollel*.

As the Yeshiva expanded, its staff increased. Reb Laib Lopian was chosen from the *kollel* to deliver a *shiur* and more *rebbeim* were still sought.

✥ Marginal Notes

I N 5709 (1948), Reb Laib Lopian wrote his brother-in-law, Rabbi Gurwicz, to join the Gateshead faculty. His acceptance not only changed his life but had a profound effect on post-war European Jewry. The students of the Gateshead Yeshiva were on a much higher level of learning than the ones he had taught for two decades in London. Only local boys attended the Etz Chaim Yeshiva in London, whereas European immigrants — who had studied in the famous *yeshivos* of Lithuania — came to Gateshead.

Shortly after Reb Leib arrived in Gateshead, Rabbi Landynsky left for America to seek medical assistance for a child. Reb Leib was never officially appointed *Rosh Yeshiva* in the absence of his predecessor, but it was clear that he was the most eminently suitable for the job.

Reb Leib once explained the expression כרחם אב על בנים — "as a father has compassion for his children" — in a way which demonstrated his conception of the role of a *rosh yeshiva:*

> *"A father's compassion for his children differs from a mother's. The emotions and reactions of a mother are triggered by what she sees and experiences in the present. A father, on the other hand, looks more into the future, which results in more calculated responses. We therefore implore the Almighty to have compassion for us as a father has for his children – compassion which takes the future into account..."*

Reb Leib viewed his students as sons and cared about them not only during their years in the Yeshiva, but long after. Their welfare was uppermost in his mind.

Reb Leib taught both in the classroom and by example. His phenomenal diligence was his primary lesson.

In his later years, he lived in a house across from the Yeshiva, where he made a point of learning in a room in which the windows faced the Yeshiva building. "I want my students to know how I spend my time," he explained. In that room the Rosh Yeshiva could be seen deeply engrossed in learning until late at night.

In fact, Reb Leib became so attached to that room that he refused to leave it even for a daily fifteen-minute walk. "Surely," his students argued, "the Rosh Yeshiva will be able to contemplate Torah thoughts as he walks — but eighteen hours of sitting every day must be unhealthy." But Reb Leib was afraid of getting stranded without a sefer in the midst of a walk — an eventuality which overrode the appeal of a stroll.

HIS YESHIVA SCHEDULE* included delivering a "blatt shiur" every day and two "inyanim shiurim" weekly to the advanced students. These *shiurim* were later transcribed and became monumental works.

Reb Leib was very meticulous about writing down his own thoughts as well as scholarly discourses which he had heard. When he was a student in "Mir" he asked visiting *talmidim* to relate *shiurim* their respective *roshei yeshiva* had delivered. In this way he assembled notebooks of lectures from that generation's leading Torah luminaries.

Opposed to the idea of young people printing *sefarim*, Reb Leib reasoned that since he was an elderly *rosh yeshiva*, he could allow himself the privilege, and published

---

* Reb Leib's dedication to the Yeshiva and to Torah study did not keep him from becoming the chairman of Agudath Israel's world organization. Even though this job entailed dozens of meetings and travelling across Europe, he never missed an appointment.

his first book in 1971. He entitled the *sefer* ראשי שערים —
Rashei Shearim, a title adapted from the name of the city
which hosted the Yeshiva: *shearim* means "gates" and *rosh*
means "head." (The "Baal HaMaor," who honored the city
which hosted *him,* provided Reb Leib with the idea.)

The *Rashei Shearim* are a collection of the *inyanim
shiurim* which he delivered at the Yeshiva. Reb Leib wrote
in his preface that he was publishing the books to serve as a
review for his *talmidim* — humble words from a man whose
works are viewed as masterpieces throughout the yeshiva
world.

In 1979, Reb Leib decided to print his *blatt shiurim.*
These lectures were recorded in the margins of his Gemara,
and for each study cycle** he used a brand new one.
Nevertheless, every page in every Gemara was crowded
with annotations.

Reb Leib's remarkable power of *chidush* — novel
thought — is demonstrated by the hundreds of original
thoughts proposed every time he relearned the same
Gemara he had studied dozens of times in the past. This
collection of *shiurim* was entitled ארזא דבי רב which means
"pillar of the *beis midrash,*" based on his name, אריה זאב.

FOR *SUKKOS* 5737 (1977), Rabbi and Rebbitzen
Gurwicz travelled to Israel to visit their children. This
was to be his last excursion in the company of his wife. On
their return trip to Gateshead the Rebbitzen suffered a
heart attack and died in Heathrow Airport. Since the
tragedy occurred on the way back from Israel, Reb Leib
understood that Providence was telling him that she should
be buried in the Holy Land.

** A five-year study cycle of nine Gemaras is standard for most yeshivos.

Rebbitzen Leiba was buried next to her father, Reb Elya Lopian, on the Mount of Olives in Jerusalem. She was honored with a large funeral and was eulogized by Reb Leib. Before he returned to England, one of his students overheard Reb Leib mutter to himself, "I must see to it that the Yeshiva lowers my salary now that I am all alone."

Two years later, Reb Leib's children recommended to their father that he marry the widow, Rebbitzen Malka Isbee. Rebbitzen Isbee had misgivings about pursuing the *shiduch*, which would entail leaving her family in Israel and relocating to dreary Gateshead. But when she learned that Reb Leib had moved on his wedding night into a home of twelve children, she realized the kind of man he must be, and that more than compensated for all the apparent drawbacks. She referred to her husband affectionately as "my *Rosh Yeshiva*."

ℛ "God, He is the Lord"

FOUR YEARS after their marriage, Reb Leib suffered a stroke. His two sons at his bedside in the Newcastle Hospital were quickly joined by their brother and sister from *Eretz Yisrael*. That afternoon the *Rosh Yeshiva* lost consciousness. The doctor in charge related that since his heart was strong, it was probable that he would remain in that condition for a long time. This news sent dozens of yeshiva students — who had arrived at the hospital — back home.

Later that Wednesday afternoon the *Mashgiach* of the Yeshiva, Rabbi Mattisyahu Salomon, joined the family and suggested that they say the verses that are recited at a deathbed. The family objected, quoting the doctor that "he will remain in that condition indefinitely." Rabbi Salomon protested that it was advisable all the same.

The sons and the *Mashgiach* and the few students who remained formed exactly a *minyan*. Together they chanted the appropriate verses — the same ones that are said at the conclusion of Yom Kippur.* With tears and sobs they began to say *Shema Yisrael*. Only a nurse was left in the room scanning the screen that monitored Reb Leib's heart.

Hashem Hu HaElokim — "God, He is the Lord." With broken hearts and unmatched fervor they repeated these words seven times, their cracked voices drowning in tears. As they recited the last verse for the seventh time, the nurse gasped and dashed out of the room.

Doctors rushed in and asked everyone to leave. Ten minutes later they emerged with word that the Rabbi had passed away. On the seventh *Hashem Hu HaElokim*, the heart monitor had stopped registering — a reflection of Reb Leib's extraordinary life.

A LL HIS life he had lived by the verse: "God, He is the Lord." The Almighty brought him to Vilkomirer, sent him across Lithuania, and led him to England.

The children decided that since their mother was buried in Jerusalem, it was appropriate for their father to be buried there as well. But the only flights to Israel were for early Thursday morning or the following Sunday. Taking the Thursday flight meant that the funeral in Gateshead would have to be very rushed and they would have to leave immediately afterwards in order to reach Heathrow Airport in time.

---

* *Shema Yisrael* is recited once; *Baruch Shem K'vod* is repeated three times; and *Hashem Hu HaElokim*, seven times.

The Gateshead Rav, however, ruled that it was wholly inappropriate to make a hasty funeral for a man who devoted his entire life for Torah. The Jerusalem burial society objected vehemently, but the Rav remained firm in his ruling that the funeral could only take place in Jerusalem on Sunday night.*

The family heeded his ruling and the first part of the funeral was scheduled for Thursday afternoon in Gateshead. In the middle of the night, Zalman Margolius, a wealthy English businessman and former student of the Gateshead Yeshiva, telephoned. "I have a Gentile friend," Margolius said, "who has several private aircraft and I told him of your dilemma. He has agreed to lend us a plane so that your father may be buried in *Eretz Yisrael* before Shabbos."

THURSDAY AFTERNOON, a massive funeral was conducted in the Gateshead Yeshiva as scheduled, and later the procession headed for Newcastle Airport, where a private Gulf Stream plane was waiting. The non-Jews of the twin cities were astounded and impressed by the size and decorum of the funeral procession.

The plane took off for Stansted Airport, Essex (London) where the *aron* was taken to a heavily attended *levaya* at the Stamford Hill *Beis Hamidrash*. The crowd was so large that many could not gain entry and stood outside in the pouring rain for over two hours. The plane then departed for *Eretz Yisrael* for the final stage of the funeral. This guaranteed that the much-desired preference for burial prior to Shabbos would be achieved.

---

* Such a lengthy delay is unheard of in Jerusalem where the deceased are buried within hours of their death.

The residents of Jerusalem were similarly responsive to the great loss. Over 15,000 people (an unusually large number for *erev Shabbos*) crowded into the Mattersdorf neighborhood of Jerusalem. The eulogies could only emphasize that which had already been said: Reb Leib stood at the helm of European Jewry by virtue of his greatness in Torah, his selfless devotion to others, his forthrightness and humility.

The honor and manner in which the funeral was conducted attested to the worth of the man. His whole life he shunned honor and therefore merited the ultimate honor. Not only was he guided by "God, He is the Lord" all his days, but he also witnessed a rich fulfillment of the Chofetz Chaim's blessing: his travelling to England was a redemption and salvation for English Jewry, as well as a fortuity which saved his own life. Even more than that, what the Gateshead *Rosh Yeshiva* accomplished in England was in the category of "Blessed be He who has compassion for the creations."

Little wonder he merited "a fair reward to those who fear Him..."

3

on Compassion

ויאמרו כל העם אשר בשער
והזקנים עדים יתן ד' את האשה
הבאה אל ביתך כרחל וכלאה
אשר בנו שתיהם את בית ישראל
ועשה חיל באפרתה וקרא שם
בבית לחם רות ד: יא

And all the people that were at the gate, and the elders, said, 'We are witnesses! May the Lord make the woman who is coming into your house like Rachel and like Leah, both of whom built up the House of Israel. May you prosper in Ephrath and be famous in Bethlehem.'

Ruth 4:11

The noblest term in the Hebrew vocabulary is רחמנות, usually defined as compassion. But with רחם — womb — as its root, a more literal translation would be "motherly love" — the only genuinely unselfish devotion. In the domain of the family and the home, which the woman was enjoined to cultivate, "Sarah's lamp burned from Shabbos to Shabbos."

The temptations to deviate from the righteous path are ever-increasing, but in each generation there have been those outstanding women in whom the virtues of the *Imahos* live on.

Her Deeds Praise Her

WHEN CHAYA LEAH Strelzer was five years old her family took leave of Aisheshok, Poland. Every Jew in the town came to bid them farewell on their journey to *Eretz Yisrael*. Before departing, Reb Eliahu Strelzer brought Chaya Leah to the Chofetz Chaim for a blessing: "May you marry a *talmid chacham* and live a long, fruitful life... I envy you, *maideleh,* for you will live in the 'Land flowing with milk and honey'..." The words of the sage were to come true in a glorious chapter of Jewish matriarchy spanning ninety-six years.

On one of Chaya Leah's father's visits to the home of the Brisker Rav, Reb Yehoshua Leib Diskin, he unwittingly initiated fulfillment of the first half of the blessing. At the same time Reb Hirsh Michel Shapiro, "the *tzadik* of Jerusalem" (see "A Time to Embrace" in *Once Upon a Soul*), was conversing with the Rav. When Reb Yehoshua Leib saw the two scholars together, he recommended in a tone more befitting a command, "Reb Hirsh Michel, you have a wonderful son, and you, Reb Eliahu, have a modest daughter — how appropriate it would be if they were to wed..."

"But she is only fourteen years old," protested Reb Eliahu, " — too young to be a mother!"

"Who can say that she will give birth right away?" responded the Brisker Rav. Reasoning like this, from such a man, was hard to dispute. The couple was married in Nissan 5649 (1889) in the home of Reb Yehoshua Leib; Chaya Leah's first of four children was born five years later...

౭౩

BATTEI MACHSE, a neighborhood noted for its proximity to the Western Wall and abundance of *tzadikim*, served a special purpose in 1929. Synagogues normally crowded with *talmidei chachamim* became hideouts for incognito members of the nascent 'Hagana' corps. Scattered among the rows of Battei Machse's shuls, the clandestine defenders could evade the ever-watchful eye of the British. In that year riots ripped through cities, and Arab guerrilla bands kept the countryside in a state of perpetual siege.

Most of the residents of Battei Machse were indifferent to the men of the Hagana. The fighters were predominantly irreligious, and the punishment for harboring an "underground member" was known to be severe. To Chaya Leah Shapiro, however, they were no different from any other Jews. She therefore cooked for them, cared for them and housed them as she did the civilian inhabitants they were sworn to defend. When in August of that year the Arab villagers of Silwan, located directly below Battei Machse, attacked their Yemenite Jewish neighbors in Mai Shiloach, the wounded and homeless found their way to Chaya Leah for shelter and food.

ONE CAN IMAGINE the tension and sense of impending doom the day the Chief British Police Officer* of Jerusalem entered the neighborhood in search

* From 1922 to 1948, Palestine was under British Mandatory rule.

of Chaya Leah Shapiro. The sheer volume of people who regularly entered her home could arouse anyone's suspicion, but it was also widely known in the community that she was privy to every Hagana-related activity.

The officer, as it turned out, had been dispatched on a peculiar mission: Chaya Leah's eldest son, Moshe Eliezer, who lived in America, hadn't heard from his parents since the outbreak of the riots early in the summer. In despair, he approached the U.S. State Department for help. The State Department telegraphed its consulate in Jerusalem which in turn contacted the police to investigate the welfare of the Shapiros.

The urgency of the request brought the case to the attention of the Chief of Police. He and his entourage trooped through Battei Machse — within arms reach of the very men they spent their days and nights trying to apprehend.

"Mrs. Shapiro," the Chief began in English. Chaya Leah retained her composure for the slightest sign of panic could precipitate an intensive interrogation. "I have been sent by the United States of America..."

"United States of America?" Could it be, she wondered, that her husband, Reb BenZion's fame had reached those distant shores? The officer, assuming from her bewilderment that Mrs. Shapiro didn't understand English, switched to German, to which she responded in Yiddish.

The awesome weight of fear fell from Chaya Leah's shoulders when she realized that all the officer wanted was for her to write a few words to her son, a note to be sent to America via diplomatic pouch. Relieved, Chaya Leah didn't waste the opportunity of meeting with the Chief; in her appealing way, she managed to exact some favors for her neighborhood while simultaneously diverting the kind officer's attention from Hagana members' whereabouts...

CHAYA LEAH'S charm and wit were irresistible — and effective: Most who entered her house ended up doing chores and never remembering how she had gotten them to help, recalling only what an enjoyable experience it had been to work in her company. Children who told their parents that they were "going outside to play" often would sneak into her home to see how they could help. Chaya Leah never looked for acclaim — but she couldn't avoid it.

Born into a distinguished rabbinic family, she was the granddaughter of Reb Shmuel Dalinover — a student of Reb Chaim Volozhiner and author of *Minchas Shmuel* on *Brachos* and *Shaarei Dim'a*. Her father, Reb Eliahu Strelzer, was the local *dayan* and *tzadik* of Aisheshok, Poland. It was his custom to enter his wife's store, empty the cash drawer without counting the amount, and disburse the money to the poor of Aisheshok. He also routinely appropriated any article of clothing that he could find in his house and used it to cover the cold *bochurim* who slept on the yeshiva's benches.

Chaya Leah's husband, Reb BenZion, was a true heir to his father, Reb Hirsh Michel Shapiro. All of Hirsh Michel's piety, saintliness, and humility was transmitted to his only son. In fact, Reb BenZion concealed his phenomenal Torah knowledge so well that his father-in-law concluded his daughter had married an ignoramus. It was only after Reb Eliahu's disappointment became public knowledge that Reb Hirsh Michel ordered his son to reveal the extent of his scholarship.

Jerusalem, better known as *Yerushalayim shel Maalah* for all of its saints and sages, was bedazzled. Whereas Reb Hirsh Michel was aware of the world around him but chose to abstain from its every pleasure, it could be said that Reb BenZion did not even know what worldly pleasure was. He barely slept and hardly ate, never took an unnecessary glance or even knew what money looked like. He spent his days wrapped in *tallis* and *tefillin* diligently learning Torah; his nights were devoted to the study of Kabbalah.

R EB BENZION'S lifeline to the physical world was Chaya Leah. Without her to keep him informed, his total absorption in his learning would have rendered him oblivious to basic human amenities. Before his marriage his clothes were often on inside out and his buttons undone. If Chaya Leah hadn't seen to it that he had supper in the evening, he would have gone to sleep without eating.

His "sleep," for lack of a better word, was a brief nap prior to leaving for shul to say *Tikun Chatzos* at midnight. Before he left, Chaya Leah would prepare a cup of coffee from concentrate she kept ready in a jar.

One night Chaya Leah wasn't feeling well and asked Reb BenZion to prepare his own cup of coffee. Early the next morning she noticed that the jar of laundry blueing – "blueyah" – was on the table and the coffee jar was still in its place! She began to tremble with apprehension and dispatched her granddaughter to the shul to check on Reb BenZion.

"Bubby, Bubby," shouted the hysterical child when she returned. "His beard is blue all around his lips and there are blue streaks running down the corners!" "Quick," implored Chaya Leah, "go call the medic and I'll meet you at the shul."

"When the medic heard that someone had swallowed laundry blueing, he jumped out of bed and ran to the shul. But when he saw who the victim was, he began to grin. "What are you smiling about?" asked a worried Chaya Leah. "You didn't tell me that it was Reb BenZion who drank the poison – I don't think that it could hurt him." And with those words he wished everyone a good morning and headed back home...

CHAYA LEAH'S home became a landmark of the old *yishuv*. On *Yom Tov*, services at the Kosel were followed by a *kiddush* at Reb BenZion's house. Every Torah notable from outside of Jerusalem or abroad invariably followed the same itinerary upon entering the Holy City: the first stop was at the Kosel; the second stop was at Reb BenZion's.

The Shapiro home was situated on the Eastern lip of Battei Machse, a two minute walk up a stone path from the Kosel. It was sparsely furnished but like an abode that one might expect to house angels. Its one and only room was limestone-white with a high arched ceiling. The walls were bare except for bunches of dates, figs, and garlic strung for drying and tied to a protruding nail. The floor, laid with smooth shiny stones, held a *kasten* — a wooden chest which doubled as a bench; a narrow pine table; two cast iron beds; and a beautifully carved, stately bookcase.

The *kasten* served as Chaya Leah's one and only closet. All the clothing and linen therein was folded neatly and compactly, and she could locate anything with ease by simply measuring the stacks. The beds — thin straw pallets covered with a white sheet, a fluffy white down quilt and over-stuffed pillows — looked more like clouds than anything else. It was under these quilts that Chaya Leah kept her soup warm on Friday nights, and it was upon these propped up pillows that Reb BenZion learned when he was confined to bed later in life. The bookcase formed a room divider behind which Reb BenZion disappeared into a world reserved for the few.

SUMMER GUESTS were treated to a cold drink which Chaya Leah fetched from her *luftshafka* — her "refrigerator in the sky." Made out of scrap wood and screening, it was a simple box suspended from the ceiling directly between the draft of the windows and door. Her kitchen, a tiny cubicle, was located outside the house, in the courtyard.

Visitors were always astounded by Chaya Leah's range of interest and breadth of knowledge. "You're from Slonim? How are the *chadorim* doing? Have they fixed the benches next to the river?" Chaya Leah remembered more about Aisheshok than more recent immigrants from her native town. She even questioned New Yorkers about their boroughs and Californians regarding their earth tremors.

After enjoying Chaya Leah's refreshment and entertaining conversation, guests would step behind the bookcase to receive a blessing from Reb BenZion. The time spent in this household would be remembered as the highlight of their trip to Jerusalem.

Invariably they would find the Shapiro home already crowded with other scholars who had come to talk with Reb BenZion, or listen to Chaya Leah. Rabbi Moshe Blau; Rabbis Aharon, Yaakov, and Raphael Katzenelenboigen; Rabbis Shimon, Chaim Yehuda, Eliezer and Yehoshua Shmidman together with Rabbi Abbish Eizen, all visited Chaya Leah regularly to hear about Reb Yehoshua Leib Diskin, Reb Yosef Chaim Zonnenfeld and others. The *gedolim* of Jerusalem *paskened maaseh ravs* exclusively according to Chaya Leah's rendition. The heads of these notables, and many others, were adorned with expertly handmade white yarmulkas which she crocheted in her spare time.

ALTHOUGH CHAYA LEAH never attended school, she had mastered a variety of disciplines. Rabbi Aryeh Levin pleaded with the family to transcribe her every word to serve as a repository of wisdom and authentic history.

Chaya Leah's words were never recorded, but her

counsel made an indelible mark on the *yishuv:* Reb BenZion didn't make a move without consulting her and even asked his wife about what to learn. Any *shalom bayis* or human relations problem came before her for arbitration — either directly or by referral from the *gedolim* of Jerusalem. Her tender, motherly nature worked in concert with her limitless patience to hear every side through.

Chaya Leah's key to successful arbitration was her well-known refusal to hear *lashon hara* — no matter what the circumstances. The parties to the dispute would be obliged to unburden themselves without attaching blame or unleashing acrimony upon their co-disputants. Handicapped by the inability to blame the other, the complainant would inevitably take upon himself the burden of guilt.

After Chaya Leah would hear the other party out under the same terms, she would comment, "It's funny that you should blame yourself, for your husband/neighbor/competitor (or whatever the case may be) also took full responsibility for the quarrel..." Chaya Leah would then declare that their differences were in one area only: which party should be condemned for causing hard feelings.

HER SAGACITY was overwhelming and her technique compelling. If Chaya Leah, the cleverest woman in all of Jerusalem couldn't find a reason to disagree, what were they bickering about?...

Chaya Leah's insight was apparent in other areas: Before rental apartments existed in Palestine, she recommended the establishment of rent-controlled neighborhoods for young couples.

Near the end of her life, when Chaya Leah was admitted to Bikur Cholim Hospital, she complained about the noise from the busy streets which surround the wards. "I told them not to build it here," she groaned in exasperation, "for this very reason!..."

CHAYA LEAH employed her wisdom most effectively in the service of kindness. With limited space and financial means, tact and diplomacy were crucial: Showering her family with perpetual benevolence was a job in itself; nonetheless she found time to devote herself to others.

Chaya Leah was always the first to assist in the absence of a natural mother. She raised several orphans in her home — children who later blossomed into distinguished *rabbonim* and *rebbitzens*. Indeed, when Chaya Leah passed away on *Chol HaMoed Sukkos,* a time barred from eulogizing except in the case of an outstanding sage, these very scholars who were brought up in the Shapiro home took the podium in Meah Shearim to mourn the loss of their surrogate mother.

CHAYA LEAH fed and hosted the poor and wretched of Jerusalem. The most impoverished residents of the city were immigrants from Spain, Morocco, Turkey, Iraq and the Balkans, who lived literally in holes in the ground between the Yochanan ben Zakkai Synagogue and the Shaar HaShamayim Yeshiva.

Every Shabbos Chaya Leah cooked an enormous *cholent.* Clearly Reb BenZion, whose only purpose in eating was to be able to make a blessing to thank Hashem (and therefore ate only the minimum required in order to do so) wouldn't consume so large a *cholent.* First, she set aside her husband's portion and enough for whomever else graced her table. Then, while the *cholent* was still hot, Chaya Leah provided room service to dozens of poor families who cherished her company as much as the meal. Her unwavering concern and involvement with those indigent families resulted in a fluency in Arabic and Spanish. On Passover, in addition to her own large family (which spanned three generations), she hosted another four such families in her one-room house.

Chaya Leah consulted her *Tehillim* and prayerbook frequently, and periodically walked to *Kever Rachel* to commune with "*Mama Rochel*," as she called her. In fact, when she first arrived in *Eretz Yisrael* at the age of five, she told her father that "we must immediately go to *Mama Rochel* and tell her: ושבו בנים לגבולם — 'Stay your voice from weeping and your eyes from tears... for your children have returned to their own boundaries!' "

Chaya Leah taught and exemplified the beauty of *tznius*. Modesty, she would emphasize, is not only the way you look *outside,* but the way you think and feel *inside.* It regulates the color and fabric of your clothing, not just its length. Modesty demands that simplicity pervade every aspect of life and home.

> *Chaya Leah always made her purchases in quantities of grams rather than kilos. The outhouse in her courtyard served all the residents of the block, but it was Chaya Leah who secretly kept it clean.*

Chaya Leah's foremost requests were חננו מאתך דעה — "Grant us from Your knowledge..." — to be blessed with knowledge and to use it properly; and אל תצריכנו... לא לידי מתנת בשר ודם ולא לידי הלואתם — "Make us not dependent on the gifts and loans of man." Her first request was granted and she was punctilious about keeping her part of the deal. Her second request was fulfilled in an existence of perpetual giving.

It pained her greatly to spend the last weeks of her life in a hospital relying upon the help of others. The doctors could not understand how a woman so old and afflicted with such an agonizing disease did not complain.

> *"Why don't I complain?" she questioned in her typical way of answering by asking. "I am old..." Chaya Leah began to reflect on all that she had witnessed in her long lifetime: pogroms and blood libels in Europe and the riots in Hebron and Jerusalem, the War of Independence, the Sinai Campaign, the War of Attrition and the Six Day War. "I am old, and now the young ר״יל are suffering – so how can I say I feel pain?"*

The hosptial staff began to appreciate that Chaya Leah was more than just an exceptional woman... She was a living tribute to the glory of Jewish motherhood and the splendor of Jerusalem.

A S A LITTLE GIRL Chaya Leah was instructed to recite Chapter 96 of *Tehillim*: "Sing to the Lord a new song..." instead of the one usually said in correlation to one's age. On the last Rosh Hashanah of her life, illness kept Chaya Leah from offering up the song she had sung everyday. She survived until *Sukkos* and reached her 96th year. It was on the 17th of Tishrei, 5731 that this song was no longer chanted by a singer whose life's lyrics were identical with those of the Psalmist: "Sing to the Lord, bless His Name, announce His salvation from day to day..."

Jerusalem was captured by Richard the Lionhearted, destroyed by Saladin, claimed by Godfrey of Buillon, rebuilt by . Egypt's Mamelukes, attacked by Suleiman the Magnificent, stormed by Napoleon, and the list goes on. But Chaya Leah and others like her were the very buttress of the Holy City. She represented an indomitability of spirit which could not be conquered by force or polluted by outside influences.

The Best Theater in Town

IMAGINE, if you will, a humble two-room home in the run-down Beis Yisrael/Meah Shearim quarter of Jerusalem. This home of meager proportions, furnished most modestly, houses a family of eleven, plus, at any given time, an indeterminate number of those less fortunate: the hungry, the impoverished of spirit, the destitute, the homeless, the infirm, the aged...

Such was the home of Malka and Reb Chaim Steinberg, who turned their simple abode into a veritable factory of benevolence and hospitality, concern and altruism.

The Steinberg home, until Malka's passing in 5733 (1973), was one of Jerusalem's best-known charitable institutions, although by no means a governmentally supported one. It owed its reputation to the lifelong devotion of its proprietress to philanthropy of every form, a devotion which found expression in the myriad acts of humankindness Malka performed throughout her years.

THE DRIVING FORCE in Malka's existence — her obsession with helping others — developed at a tender age. When she was still a young girl, she discovered an elderly woman living alone in a bleak, fetid hovel. Many who would have helped this woman were put off by the stench of putrefaction that emanated from her house and the foul debris and muck that littered the dismal tenement. But Malka was undaunted: singlehandedly, yet cheerfully, she set about her private renewal project. Later, others older and more qualified followed Malka's lead and helped to complete the rehabilitation job.

As a mere teenager, Malka chose to devote her time and energy not to frivolous play with friends but to providing food and drink to the indigent who gathered in the streets. She also sought out mothers who had just given birth and assisted them by serving three meals a day while simultaneously babysitting for their older children. By the age of fifteen, Malka was a one-woman mobile convalescent home.

It must have been around that time that dispensing food became her *raison d'être*. When people are hungry, she reasoned, they can neither concentrate on serving the Almighty nor lead a happy life.

In the presence of Malka Steinberg the very first priority was eating. She wouldn't allow someone in her home without having him make a *bracha*; outside, she was always equipped with food and drink.

Every erev Rosh Chodesh, *Malka travelled to Kever Rachel. The infrequent buses to Bethlehem were inevitably packed with irate, thirsty travellers, drained by the slow, fatiguing trip. But Malka always came prepared. Who else would have thought of*

> *bringing refreshments for a whole bus-load? Who else*
> *would insist that every passenger — including the bus*
> *driver — partake of her food and juice before they visit*
> *the* Kever?

Malka's obsession with providing food found repeated justification. In 1948 when there was talk of Independence, a British evacuation — and war, Malka wasted no time listening to the radio or collecting gossip on the streets: she was too busy converting her home into a storehouse.

Yosef HaTzadik (the "Provider") would have been proud. Sack upon sack of wheat, flour, rice, beans, nuts, and other staples were hauled into her courtyard. The house began to look like a battlefield itself with the bags forming labyrinthine partitions through the rooms. The bureaus were glutted with cans and preserves. In short, the Steinberg home was stocked for a decade-long seige. Malka wasn't preparing just for her family — she never did. Somehow she knew, intuitively perceived, that all of Jerusalem would need her help, and the opportunity to help others was an "offer she couldn't refuse..."

O NE MORNING Malka spotted a boy passing by the courtyard in front of her home on his way to yeshiva. "He looks like he would be able to learn better if he'd eat a good breakfast," she thought to herself. The next morning, Malka laid an ambush and first commanded him, then, when that didn't work, begged and pleaded with him to have a cup of milk and egg which she had prepared. Thirty years later, this boy — now a distinguished *talmid chacham* — confessed to her family sitting *shiva* over her passing, that it was Malka's nutritious breakfasts that enabled him to continue in yeshiva. "I am who I am today, thanks to Rebbitzen Steinberg's incessant persuasion and remarkable perception..."

Perception, if not clairvoyance, was a keystone of her character.

> *An Australian* baal teshuva *once appeared at her door hoping to find someone to whom he could relate. One would hardly have imagined an elderly second-generation Jerusalemite to be the most suitable conversationalist for a young man from such a diverse background. But when Malka began to unravel the boy's past in minute detail simply by looking at his face, he felt as though he were conversing with a lifelong, intimate friend.*

Everyone was aware of Malka's keen insight — some were even frightened by it. But they had nothing to fear: She used her perspicacity as a kindly tool, not as a weapon:

> *When it came to hosting her guests, who always numbered in double digits, Malka didn't offer them all identical servings or even portions of the same dish. "Why do you vary the menu so at one meal?" people asked.*
>
> *"Because he likes his food cooked this way and she doesn't care for this dish; he shouldn't eat salt," and so on. She always knew.*

When engaged in a mitzva Malka didn't probe people's past. "Right now it's not my business, and knowing too much may hamper my performance..." And that was the greatest prohibition. Malka Steinberg was a mistress of expediency. She managed to enlist all types of resources and manpower for the cause.

Her star recruit, however, was her husband, who had been a pampered only-child from a relatively well-to-do family. He had never envisioned sharing such a life or living in such a home, but he learned fast and eventually even outdid his wife in generosity.

FORTY YEARS AGO *shlissel gelt* — "key-money" apartments (wherein lease agreements provide lifetime protection of the lessee's housing rights) did not exist in Jerusalem. It wasn't uncommon for tenants to be peremptorily evicted onto the streets — that is, until Malka Steinberg rounded them up into her two-room apartment. Where did the orphan-survivors of the Holocaust stay? At Malka's, of course. After the pogrom in Hebron, the wounded needed a place to recuperate; a Russian family with nine children, from the time they arrived in Israel, were unable to find proper accommodations; all of them came to the Steinbergs — who had nine children of their own.

The children slept in their beds in perpendicular formation with their feet, and many others, resting on a bench. The Steinberg children never knew who would be their bed mates on any particular night. But they loved it, and claimed they couldn't sleep any other way. Their mother and father had long-since given up their own beds for guests and they themselves slept on a bench.

Malka's home looked like a cross between a dormitory and a pajama party. Frequently the guests included new mothers (whose babies had been born at the Steinbergs') and they required a crib adjacent to their beds. Every morning Reb Chaim had to engage in delicate acrobatic feats, entailing laborious furniture moving and redesign, just to repair out the front door for his sunrise *minyan*. But he never complained.

One afternoon, Reb Chaim's mechutan found him sitting on the broad windowsill — which doubled as a bed at night — at the entrance to the house. "Why don't you sit at the table?" asked his mechutan. "The table is for the guests," Reb Chaim responded, as he motioned for his mechutan to join him on the sill.

HOW DID MALKA manage to house and provide for so many guests? No one knows. It was as if the miracles and blessings of Jerusalem (*Pirkei Avos*, 5:8), "The people stood closely pressed together and yet found ample space to prostrate themselves; no man ever said to his fellow: 'There is too little room for me to lodge overnight in Jerusalem' " were imbued in her walls.

But her home was more than a hostel. During the day it doubled as a day care center, drop-in center, refuge for battered wives, social hall, place to unburden oneself and psychiatrist's office, to name but a few services. All of the "rejects" and misfits of the city found their way to Rebbitzen Malka. "The more affluent, more fortunate people can take care of themselves," she would say.

Malka understood that often, more than a good meal, people needed a good *shmooze*. So she gave both — she would give anything to gratify. Malka would lecture, relate stories, tell jokes, listen to problems and often sing to women who found her sweet, melodious voice soothing and relaxing. She mended and bolstered shattered egos and wouldn't let a troubled visitor leave until his spirits were lifted.

Malka's guests could be boisterous or taciturn, self-respecting or self-effacing. Many of them brought their ponderous physical and emotional burdens with them. To afford her guests the personal attention they sought, she was compelled on occasion, to divide them between her two rooms. If "honor struggles" or inter-guest bickering still prevailed, she would devise different techniques. And even when each guest finally felt "at home" and content in his particular corner, Malka continued shuttling back and forth and catering to make sure that they all remained pleased. "This is the best theater in town," she would boast, referring to the variety of colorful characters who graced her home.

A LL WHO CROSSED her threshold, even the daily drop-ins (let alone the overnight, over-week or over-year guests), felt that her home was theirs. Malka's ever-abiding care and succor made it impossible to feel otherwise. And this service was available to even the most daunting clients.

The Belzer Rebbe advised a Tel Aviv woman to remove her severely retarded and handicapped daughter from an insane asylum to a private home in the hope that such an environment might provide more effective therapy. Naturally this woman brought her daughter — her only child — to Malka, as though it were understood from the Rebbe's instructions.

After greeting the woman, Rebbitzen Steinberg summoned a specialist from Shaare Zedek Hospital to examine the child. The doctor asked the girl's mother if she had any other children. "*Nein,*" she replied, but the doctor misconstrued her answer to mean *nine* children. "Then may you have *nachas* from the other eight," he wished her as he stepped out the door. Seeing the hurt and dejection which gripped the mother, Malka accepted both into her home.

For once the Steinberg children objected. The girl rampaged through the house, wasn't toilet trained, and was dreadful in appearance because of pronounced deformities. Yet Malka refused to budge from her commitment. One day, however, in a moment of weakness, Malka agreed to rent a nearby apartment for the girl and her mother at her own expense. Malka's kitchen and hospitality, of course, remained at their disposal.

An elderly lady who had never married moved into the Steinbergs'. She had no compunctions about living there rent-free for Malka feigned seeking her hoary counsel before taking any decision.

&

An aging Rebbitzen who knocked on the Steinberg door one freezing winter morning, found her shoes whisked off her feet and toes soaking in warm water before she could even remember saying hello.

THE DOZENS of people who gravitated to Malka's home bore testimony to her *Weltanschauung*. She contended that if you truly wish to do a mitzva, you don't have to look for one — it will find you. Each mitzva is nothing less than a Divine summons, and if you fail to answer "the call" you may not be offered the privilege of another mission. Furthermore, the agreement to perform a mitzva implies undertaking the whole job. Abandoning the mission halfway is a dereliction of duty.

How much more so is this true for a woman, whose very existence on earth was predicated on performing acts of kindness and related mitzvos. A woman, Malka claimed, must be stronger and more active than a man. She must know the *siddur* by heart so that she can have prayers on her lips as she cooks, cleans and does her chores.

Rebbitzen Steinberg lived by her words. She saw to the marriage of the orphans the Steinbergs adopted, that is, found their match, tended to the wedding and arranged housing. During the War of Independence, she gathered into her well-stocked home four families whose homes were exposed to enemy bombardment. When someone came to the door, her only question was how she could help. Even Arab workers knew to head for her home for a hearty meal.

But Malka's kindness was by no means restricted to the home; her house was merely a base. When she heard, for example, of a man who was inordinately miserly with household expenses, she smuggled in daily meals to his wife and children. Every morning Malka dispatched gallons of piping hot tea to the Etz Chaim *cheder* so that the *melamdim* who taught and sang to the boys wouldn't lose their voices.

MALKA'S ABILITY to dispense food didn't come from a personal overabundance. The Steinbergs' sole income was the money Reb Chaim eked out from his humble fruit stand. To cover Malka's huge budget and food demand, she borrowed staggering sums of money from "free loan societies" and collected left-over food scraps from yeshivos and *Talmud Torah*s. It was common knowledge in Beis Yisrael that any unwanted or left-over food was to be donated to the Steinberg kitchen, where the food was put to good use. In sum — the Lord provided.

Malka once came across a dejected-looking, woman sitting on the sidewalk. "What's the matter?" she asked with concern.

"I'm waiting for Elijah the Prophet," the lady retorted and returned to her sulking.

"Well, I'm certainly not Elijah," started Malka, sensing that a mitzva was about to fall into her lap, "but maybe I can help."

"Only if you're a millionaire you can... I have no money to marry off my daughter and therefore cannot find her a match. She is getting older and I am getting desperate."

"Don't worry," Malka assured her and headed off

to begin campaign number who-knows-what. Malka turned to her relatives, friends, neighbors, and every available free loan society — and money began to materialize.

The next day Malka found this lady just as she had left her: disheartened and despondent — grief incarnate — waiting for salvation to appear out of nowhere. And it did. "She was truly my Elijah the Prophet," related this woman to her friends.

THE STEINBERGS were beloved heroes of Jerusalem's Sefardi residents. Many Sefardi parents introduced their children as "hers" — pointing to Malka Steinberg. She reared them, fed them, looked after them, waited with them at clinics, brought them to doctors, and saw to it that they didn't abandon the path of their fathers. When Reb Chaim passed away six years before his wife in 5727 (1967) dozens of Sefardi teenagers and adults walked after his bier, crying *"Tatee, Tatee!"*

Malka assigned one of her grandsons to bring meals to a well-to-do Sefardi merchant. When the boy first started making his deliveries, people protested that the merchant was a wealthy man and did not have to live off contributions. Rebbitzen Steinberg countered that the man was actually a masochistic miser and did not even buy for himself essential food provisions. "How can stashed money alleviate starvation? Go, my grandson, go, and don't listen to others. Your job is to see to it that his man eats."

The week that Malka returned her soul to its Maker, the merchant died of hunger...

Malka managed to get her whole family into the act. Because of an argument between her husband's family and herself over which school the Steinberg daughters should attend, the girls ended up not going to any school at all. But this didn't create a truancy problem. Had they gone to school, they would never have had time for their studies for they were already enrolled in Malka's "*Chessed* University" around the clock.

During the day, they were assigned to take children outside to play to relieve overburdened mothers. Curricula often included field trips, *i.e.*, packing lunches and walking youngsters from congested homes to the Shmuel HaNavi Street area, which was as yet undeveloped. Malka's daughters would park their entourage next to the *cheder* located on Shmuel HaNavi so that they could be serenaded by the sounds of Torah-learning while breathing the open air. At night there were other duties and chores which had to be performed more discreetly. And of course, there was always "homework."

MALKA FASTED frequently (which may have caused her discomfort but never hindered her *chessed* activities), praying that her children develop into God-fearing *bnei Torah*. Her supplications were answered: every one of her nine children either became a *talmid chacham* or married one.

Rebbitzen Steinberg was an "innovator" in the realm of *chessed* and each one of her children inherited a different portion of her special legacy. She was one of the first in Jerusalem, for example, to open a *gemach* — free loan society — for dishes, silverware, pots, etc. One daughter inherited and expanded this *gemach*, while another child continues to let low-rental apartments for the needy. Yet another child is heir to Malka's propensity for arranging *shiduchim* — finding suitable matches for men and women.

Malka never yelled at her children or disciplined them in a stern way. But she also didn't spoil them. Actually, she viewed everyone who entered her home or whom she encountered, as her own child. The only difference between her biological children and others was that she turned her own offspring into collaborators in her mission. Whenever she would meet a *gadol* or a *rebbe* she would — unlike most mothers — never ask for a blessing for her own children but rather request that she should be successful in her mitzvos.

Her giving and concern became the very fabric of her nature. When she was admitted to the hospital towards the end of her life, she refused to eat until all the trays of the other patients in her ward were emptied and their needs seen to.

Malka Steinberg lived at a time when there was no jealousy — for there was little to be jealous about. A person owned one dress, one pair of shoes, one kerchief and no more. Her house was one of nothing — two bare rooms with a kitchen and a bathroom located outside — and everything. Malka had an uncanny knack for knowing how, where and whom to help. As long as there was someone, somewhere, unhappy with life, he or she was a likely objective for benevolence from the saint of Beis Yisrael.

Duty Was Joy

T O TRAVEL from Germany to Palestine in 1916 via war-torn Europe was unusual, but then, so was the traveller. Selma Mayer was bound for *Eretz Yisrael,* by invitation, or more correctly, by conscription of Dr. Moshe Wallach, founder and director of Shaare Zedek Hospital.

It was appropriate for the first Jewish hospital established outside the walls of the Old City to have as its Head Nurse one of the first Jewish women to have passed the German State Nursing examinations. But what prompted Schwester* Selma to leave a coveted position at Solomon Heine Hospital in Hamburg? The same motivation which had inspired her to become a nurse. When Selma was only five years old, her mother passed away. She felt the loss so deeply that she decided to devote her life to providing that which she herself had so desperately missed — motherly love.

The realization of this goal became a legend that spanned nearly seven decades. Selma's first night at Shaare

---

* The German *schwester* (pronounced *shvester*, like its Yiddish cognate), meaning "sister," is the designation for "nurse," especially "head nurse."

Zedek (a small, rudimentary hospital built in 1902), where she was to spend the rest of her life, was also her first night with bed bugs. This was no more than a minor nuisance, she quickly discovered, in a city plagued with typhus and meningitis.

TO BATTLE the city-wide epidemics was her very first assignment. With only a forty-bed, disorganized medical facility at her disposal and a chronic shortage of qualified personnel, Selma set about the task with pad and pen in hand and wrote down everything that was not in order. German-Jewish by birth, and certainly by nature, she soon whipped the hospital into shape.

The many German terms and expressions that are still part of Shaare Zedek's hospital jargon are evidence of her imprint. Every operating room appliance and apparatus is better-known by its German name: for example, a surgical clamp is called a "klammer," sponge tongs are "tuch klammers," and a "sonde" is a gastro-intestinal tube. All of the nurses soon learned they had to do "staub" — dusting — in the wards or else incur Schwester's wrath.

The greatest demand placed on Schwester Selma was that of working together with Dr. Wallach — a job which included making the rounds twice daily to every bed in the hospital, carrying out numerous errands outside the hospital premises, and maintaining the religious character of Shaare Zedek. On the side, she assumed the role of head nurse, operating room nurse, midwife, cook, sanitation supervisor, and any other position that needed filling.

DR. WALLACH ran a tight ship. Nurses weren't permitted to leave the hospital grounds without his written consent, and those who succeeded in obtaining a pass were obliged to return no later than eight P.M. Dr. Wallach regularly stood guard at the hospital gate at this hour to ascertain that the nurses returned on time.

On one such evening, a visitor pleaded to be admitted to see her husband who had just undergone an operation. "Hurry, let me in before that *meshugenah* Wallach comes along," she implored. Dr. Wallach agreed to escort her to the ward for a brief visit and after a few minutes asked her to leave. As she approached the gate, she thanked him profusely and said, "You've been so kind and helpful. What is your name?" "I'm that '*meshugenah* Wallach,' " he replied.

Such moments of levity were rare in the early years of Shaare Zedek. Almost every Jerusalem family was hungry and disease was rampant. The hospital wasn't equipped with running water, and kerosene lamps served the double function of lighting the halls and heating the rooms. A small herd of cows, which provided milk for the patients, was kept in the hospital courtyard. There too Schwester Selma tended a bonfire for sterilizing instruments.

Kashrus in the kitchen was as important to Selma as sterility in the operating rooms. Her attention to the patients' religious needs far exceeded Dr. Wallach's orders and her contribution to keeping Jerusalem's one truly religious hospital observant, was immeasurable. At her own initiative, she saw to it that men and women were seated separately in the waiting rooms. On *Purim* she arranged for everyone to hear the *Megilla* reading, arrangements which often disrupted the entire hospital just to accommodate the patients' and readers' schedules. If a man were unable to lay *tefillin* by himself, Schwester Selma was usually aware of the problem even before the patient mentioned it and was an expert at making *"tefillin shiduchim"* (the more able-bodied to help the less so) every morning.

Well before *Pesach*, Selma made sure that every patient had a *Seder* plate, and even more than that. Each year she declined the numerous offers extended by friends and former patients to join them for *Seder*. "My duty is to be with the patients," Selma explained and did all she could to make their *Seder* as joyous as possible.

I N 1934, Schwester Selma founded the Shaare Zedek Nursing School. Dr. Wallach initially opposed the plan, fearing that the school would place too much emphasis on theory instead of practical application. He later regretted his resistance (How could a school with Selma at its head be impractical?) and awarded his accolades to the school, one of Israel's finest institutions.

Schwester Selma's students learned that being a nurse entails far more than changing sheets and intravenous bottles, filling out forms and providing physical care. She taught them that just as viruses and bacteria cause disease, so can depression and heartache, but these can often be cured with heavy doses of cheerfulness and commiseration. She maintained that no effort should be spared to diminish a patient's suffering.

It was unthinkable to be tired in Schwester Selma's presence. She required everyone to work at least eighteen hours a day — as she herself did. In the 'thirties, Selma scheduled twelve-hour night shifts with only two days off each month. A few years later, the nurses rebelled, demanding eight-hour night shifts, no more than three weeks per month.

Selma was furious. How dare nurses fight for better

working conditions? "What is this, the *Histadrut* [Labour Federation]?" She contended that labor and wage disputes were anathema to the nursing profession. Monetary considerations had no place in a field of endeavor she viewed as a "calling."

Selma expected every nurse to share her sense of responsibility and devotion to duty. While entitled under her contract to a three-month vacation in Germany every three years, Schwester Selma took advantage of this option only twice in her long career. She never married. Nevertheless, she adopted three girls whose families had abandoned them in the hospital.

THE OUTBREAK of a polio epidemic in the early 1950s was a severe trial of Selma's and her students' competence and stamina. The cumbersome and complicated iron lungs, which saved the lives of so many children, required around-the-clock, expert supervision. Staff was almost impossible to find because strict Health Ministry regulations prohibited young nurses* from working in polio wards.

Schwester Selma and a small group of older nurses worked rotation shifts in Shaare Zedek's tiny isolation pavilion (the only one in Jerusalem), until the epidemic was finally brought under control. When Dr. Jonas Salk, father of the polio vaccine, visited Shaare Zedek, he was astounded that so much had been accomplished under such primitive conditions.

THE MOVE from the old Shaare Zedek facilities on Jaffa Road to the new complex in the Bayit Vegan neighborhood of Jerusalem was a transition tinged with

* Teenagers and young adults were also susceptible to poliomyelitis.

sadness for Schwester Selma. It meant not only departing from her room in the hospital where she had lived for sixty-four years, but also a departure from her unconventional doctrine of medical care.

Her old lodgings, like the hospital itself, were cramped and austerely furnished. But Selma's presence turned it into a cozy haven for patients who frequently visited to enjoy some freshly-brewed tea or even a glass of wine to help them fall asleep.

Selma's new quarters were spacious, antiseptic, and worst of all — modern. The scourge of modernity, she felt, lowered the level of health care and severed the bonds of human warmth. It created an atmosphere that was not conducive to training nurses whose sole concern was their patients' welfare.

To a certain degree, Schwester Selma was right; dedication like hers is a thing of the past. A 1975 *Time* magazine cover story on "living saints" described her as an angel, "a woman who serves God by helping man and serves man by helping God."

She knew of no other way to do her job. Her life maxim was set forth in a verse by the Nobel prize-winning Indian poet, Rabindranath Tagore, a copy of which hung on the wall above her desk.

> *I slept and dreamt that life was joy.*
> *I awoke and saw that life was duty.*
> *I acted and behold –*
> *Duty was Joy.*

ON FRIDAY, *Rosh Chodesh Adar I*, 5744 (February 3, 1984), Schwester Selma celebrated her hundredth birthday. The following Sunday was designated as a special day in Shaare Zedek for official tribute to

Schwester Selma. Early that morning, Selma Mayer returned her soul to its Maker.

All those who had intended to participate in the festive ceremony found themselves joining a funeral procession instead. Cabinet ministers, doctors, nurses, and generations of patients came to pay tribute to a legendary woman for whom duty was indeed joy.

Glossary

The following glossary provides a partial explanation of some of the foreign words and phrases used in this book. The spelling, tense and explanations reflect the way the specific word is used in *Soul Survivors*. Often, there are alternate spellings and meanings for the words. Foreign words and phrases which are immediately followed by a translation in the text are not included in this section.

ACH DU LIEBER — (Ger.) Oh, my dear!

AGUNA — lit. a "chained woman;" refers to a woman whose marriage has been terminated *de facto*, but not *de jure*, and who is therefore forbidden to remarry because she is still technically married to her absent husband.

ALIYAH — going up; term used in connection with 1. being called up to the reading of the Torah; 2. immigration to Israel

ANSHULDIGT — (Yid.) excuse me

APIKORES — heretic

ARON KODESH — lit. holy ark; ark containing the Torah scrolls

A SACH NACHAS — (Yid.) much joy

ASHREI YOSHVEI VEISECHA — lit. Happy are those who dwell in Your house; the introductory words to the *Mincha* service.

AUFRUF — (Yid.) the calling up to the Torah of the bridegroom on the Sabbath preceding his wedding

BAALEI BATIM — lay individuals

BAAL TEFILLA — leader of prayer

BAAL TESHUVA (f. BAALAS TESHUVA) — penitent who has returned to religious observance

BAITEL — (Yid.) enclosure

BAKSHEESH — (Arab., colloq.) bribe

BARUCH SHEM K'VOD — Blessed be the Name of His glorious majesty; the silent verse said immediately after SHEMA YISRAEL

BEIS DIN — court of Jewish law

BEIS HAMUSSAR — house or room devoted to MUSSAR study

BEIS MIDRASH — house of study used for both Torah study and prayer

BEKESHE — caftan

BEREISHIS — the first book of the Torah. Its name is derived from its first word — *bereishis*, lit. in the beginning

BIMA — platform located in the center of the synagogue, from where the Torah is read

BITTE — (Ger.) please

BNEI TORAH — lit. sons of Torah; men imbued with Torah teaching and values

BOCHUR (BOCHURIM) — unmarried yeshiva student

BRACHA — blessing

BRIS — the Jewish rite of circumcision

CHABUSHA — (Arab.) apple

CHACHAM — wise man; "rabbi" in Sephardic circles

CHALILAH — God forbid (idiom)

CHARGILLA — (Arab.) waterpipe

CHAZZAN — cantor; the leader of public worship

CHEDER (CHADORIM) — elementary school for religious studies

CHESSED — deeds of lovingkindness

CHEVRA KADISHA — lit. holy society; a group which provides for the religious needs of the community, particularly in the area of the care and rites of the dead

CHILLUL HASHEM — desecration of God's name

CHILLUL SHABBOS — desecration of the Shabbos

CHINUCH — education

CHOFETZ CHAIM — saintly scholar and renowned author

CHOK — popular name for *Chok LeYisrael,* an anthology of holy writings divided into daily portions to be studied throughout the year

CHOLENT — (Yid.) traditional stew prepared on Friday afternoon and kept hot until the midday Shabbos meal

CHOL HAMOED — the Intermediate Days of SUKKOS and PESACH

CHOSSAN — bridegroom

CHUMASH — set of the five books of the Torah; any of the five books

DANKE SCHON — (Ger.) thank you

DAVEN — (Yid.) pray

DAYAN — rabbinical court judge

DIN TORAH — case brought for adjudication according to Torah law

DUCHENING — blessing of the nation by descendants of Aaron's priestly family

DUMMKOPF — (Ger.) dumbbell

ERETZ YISRAEL — the land of Israel

EREV — eve

FLEISH — meat

FRAULEIN — (Ger.) Miss; an unmarried woman

GADOL (GEDOLIM) — lit. great one, refers to a giant in Torah scholarship

GA'ON — lit. brilliant one; title of honor for a distinguished sage

GELT — (Yid.) money

GEMARA — 1. commentary on the Mishna (together they comprise the Talmud) 2. a volume of the Talmud

GEMILUT CHASSADIM — performance of acts of CHESSED

GOTT IN HIMMEL — (Ger.) God in Heaven

HAISE VANT — (Yid.) hot wall

HASHEM — lit. the Name; respectful reference to God

HAVDALAH — lit. separation; service to conclude the Shabbos

HERR BARON — (Ger.) honored sir (honorific for nobility)

HESDER — combined program of yeshiva study and military service in the Israeli army

ILLUI — genius, towering Torah scholar

INYANIM SHIURIM — SHIURIM on Talmudic topics

JIRNE — (Arab.) flute

KABBALAH — the body of Jewish mystical teachings

KAMEAH — (Aram.) handwritten blessing in the form of an amulet, pendant or wall hanging

KAPITL (KAPITLACH) — (Yid.) small sections

KASHRUS — Jewish dietary law

KAVANA — devotion, intent, concentration, purpose

KETUBA — the Jewish marriage contract

KEVER RACHEL — tomb of Rachel

KIDDUSH — sanctification; prayer recited over wine to usher in the Sabbath and festivals

KIPPA (KIPPOT) — skullcap; head covering worn by religious Jews

KITTEL — white cloak donned by the CHAZZAN on High Holy Days and other festivals and by married men on various festivals and occasions according to custom

KOHEIN (KOHANIM) — a male descendant from the priestly family of Aaron

KOLLEL — post-graduate YESHIVA in which student body is usually comprised of young married students who receive stipends

KOSEL (HAMAARAVI) — lit. Western Wall; last remaining wall of the Temple courtyard and eminent holy site

LA BES — (Fr.-Arab.) Hello

LASHON HARA — evil talk; a derogatory or damaging statement about someone

LECHEM MISHNA — two loaves of bread (*challah*) eaten during Sabbath meals

LEVAYA — funeral

MAARIV — evening prayer

MAASEH RAV — lesson derived from a scholar's behavior

MAGEN DOVID — star of David

MAHN — manna which sustained the Children of Israel in the wilderness

MAIDELEH — little girl

MAMMA ROCHEL — (Yid.) Mother Rachel

MARCHABA — (Arab.) greetings!

MARCHABTAIN — (Arab.) reply to MARCHABA

MASECHES — talmudic tractate

MASHGIACH — dean of students in a yeshiva who acts as a spiritual guide and adviser

MAZEL — luck; fortune

MECHITZA — partition separating the men from the women in a synagogue

MECHUTAN — the father-in-law of one's son or daughter

MEGILLA — the scroll of Esther read in the synagogue on *Purim*

MEIN — (Ger.) my

MESHULACH — lit. messenger; itinerant fundraiser for a charitable institution

MESHUMAD — convert from Judaism

MIKDASH ME'AT — lit. small Sanctuary; synagogue

MIKVAH (MIKVAOS) — a ritual bath used for the purpose of ritual purification

MINCHA — the afternoon prayer service

MINYAN (MINYANIM) — quorum of ten adult Jewish males; the basic unit of community for certain religious purposes, including prayer

MI SHEBAIRACH — lit. the One Who blessed; the traditional prayer said as part of services for the sick and on other occasions

MISHNA (MISHNAYOS) — the earliest codification of Jewish oral law by Rabbi Yehudah Hanassi

MITZVA (MITZVOS) — lit. commandments; applied to good deeds

MODIM — lit. we give thanks; prayer of thanksgiving said while standing or bowing in gratitude to HASHEM

MUSSAR — 1. school of thought emphasizing ethical perfection; 2. moral teachings; 3. ethical lecture

NACHAS — l. joy; 2. positive fulfillment

NEBACH — (Yid.) unfortunately

NEIN — (Yid.; Ger.) no

NICHT WAHR — (Ger.) is that not so?

OBERLEUTNANT — (Ger.) first lieutenant

OIY VEY'S MEER — (Yid.) oh, agony!

ORACH CHAIM — section of the SHULCHAN ARUCH which deals with daily life

PESACH — Passover

PSAK — halachic decision

PSHAT — simple interpretation; meaning

PUSHKA — charity box

RABBONIM — rabbis

REBBE (REBBEIM) — 1. rabbi, usually a Talmud teacher; 2. instructor; 3. chassidic leader

REBBITZEN — rabbi's wife

RIBBONO SHEL OLAM — lit. Master of the Universe; God

ROSH CHODESH — beginning of the month

ROSH HASHANAH — beginning of the Jewish year

ROSH KOLLEL — KOLLEL dean

ROSH YESHIVA (ROSHEI YESHIVA) — yeshiva dean

SCHWEINHUND — (Ger.) swine hound

SEFER (SEFARIM) — book of religious content

SHABBOS — Sabbath

SHAILA (SHAILOS) — lit. question; halachic query

SHALOM ALEICHEM — lit. "peace be upon you;" traditional greeting

SHALOM BAYIS — harmony in the household

SHAS — the Talmud

SHEMA YISRAEL — prayer recited daily proclaiming the oneness of God and affirming faith in Him and His Torah

SHEMONEH ESREI — lit. eighteen; the central prayer in Jewish liturgy which is recited three times daily

SHIDUCH (SHIDUCHIM) — a (matrimonial) match

SHIUR (SHIURIM) — Torah lecture

SHIVA — lit. seven, the seven-day period of mourning

SHOFAR — ram's horn

SHTENDER — lectern, used in place of desks in many yeshivos

SHTETL — (Yid.) village

SHTIEBEL (SHTIEBLACH) — (Yid.) small, informal, intimate room for prayer or study

SHUK — (Arab.) open-air market

SHUL — (Yid.) synagogue

SHULCHAN ARUCH — code of Jewish law compiled by Rabbi Yosef Karo

SIDDUR — prayer book

SIFREI KODESH — holy books; see SEFER

SIMCHA — lit. joy; celebration

SOFER — scribe

SUKKOS — seven day festival starting on the fifteenth of Tishrei

TALLIS — four-cornered prayer shawl with fringes at each corner worn by men during morning prayers

TALMID — student

TALMID CHACHAM (TALMIDEI CHACHAMIM) — Torah scholar

TALMUD TORAH — 1. study of Torah; 2. Jewish school on an elementary level

TASHMISHEI KEDUSHA — religious articles

TATEE — (Yid.) Daddy

TEFILLA (TEFILLOS) — prayer

TEFILLIN — black leather boxes containing verses from the Bible bound to the arm and head of a man during morning prayer

TEFILLIN SHEL ROSH — TEFILLIN placed on the head

TEFILLIN SHEL YAD — TEFILLIN placed on the upper arm

TEHILLIM — Psalms

TESHUVA — lit. return; repentance

TIKUN CHATZOS — midnight prayers mourning the destruction of the Temple and imploring its restoration

TISHA B'AV — the ninth day of the month of Av; fast day commemorating the destruction of both the First and Second Temple

TIZKEH L'MITZVOT — may you be privileged to perform more MITZVOS

TOSEFOS — early annotations and commentaries to the Talmud

TREIFA — lit. torn; non-kosher; unacceptable

TZADIK (TZADIKIM) — righteous man

TZEDAKA — charity

VERZEIHUNG — (Ger.) pardon

VOUS HEIRTSACH — (Yid.) what's doing?

WUNDERBAR — (Ger.) wonderful

YEIHARAIG VE'AL YAAVOR — refers to one of the three cardinal sins where the Torah mandates that the Jew must lay down his life rather than violate the commandment

YERUSHALAYIM SHEL MAALAH — lit. Jerusalem of above; refers to an era when Jerusalem's residents were pious individuals

YESHIVA (YESHIVOS) — academy of Torah study

YESHIVA KETANA — YESHIVA for young teenagers

YINGELEH — (Yid.) little boy

YISHUV — lit. settlement; refers to early settlement of Jews in ERETZ YISRAEL

YIZKOR — prayer said on the three festivals in memory of deceased relatives

YOM TOV — holiday

ZECKEL — (Yid.) bag

ZETZ — (Yid.) slam

ZIONI — (m.) Zionist

ZOCHEH — merit